"INSIGHTFUL...ENTERTAINING...A REMINDER OF HOW MUCH WE OWE OUR FOREFATHERS."

–Richard Beeman, author of
Plain, Honest Men: The Making of the American Constitution

"*INVENTING AMERICA* IS A TERRIFIC WAY TO INTRODUCE OUR NATION'S FOUNDERS TO A NEW GENERATION OF AMERICANS."

—Gleaves Whitney, presidential historian

At the close of the Constitutional Convention of 1787 in Philadelphia an elderly woman approached Benjamin Franklin as he was leaving the Pennsylvania State House. "Tell me, Dr. Franklin," she said, "do we have a republic or a monarchy?" Dr. Franklin replied: "A republic, madam, if you can keep it."

What would our Founding Fathers think if they could see our country today? Would they turn over in their graves? Or would they be astonished that our republic is still alive? George Washington, who presided at the 1787 convention, predicted it wouldn't last twenty years, so take a guess.

Inventing America: Conversations with the Founders takes you behind the scenes of the creation of the Declaration of Independence, the U.S. Constitution, and the Bill of Rights. See how these are not just dusty old parchments stored away in a museum but how they define us as Americans and serve as a beacon of democracy to the world.

MILTON J. NIEUWSMA is a two-time Emmy Award-winning writer and creator of the PBS series *Inventing America: Conversations with the Founders.*

INVENTING America

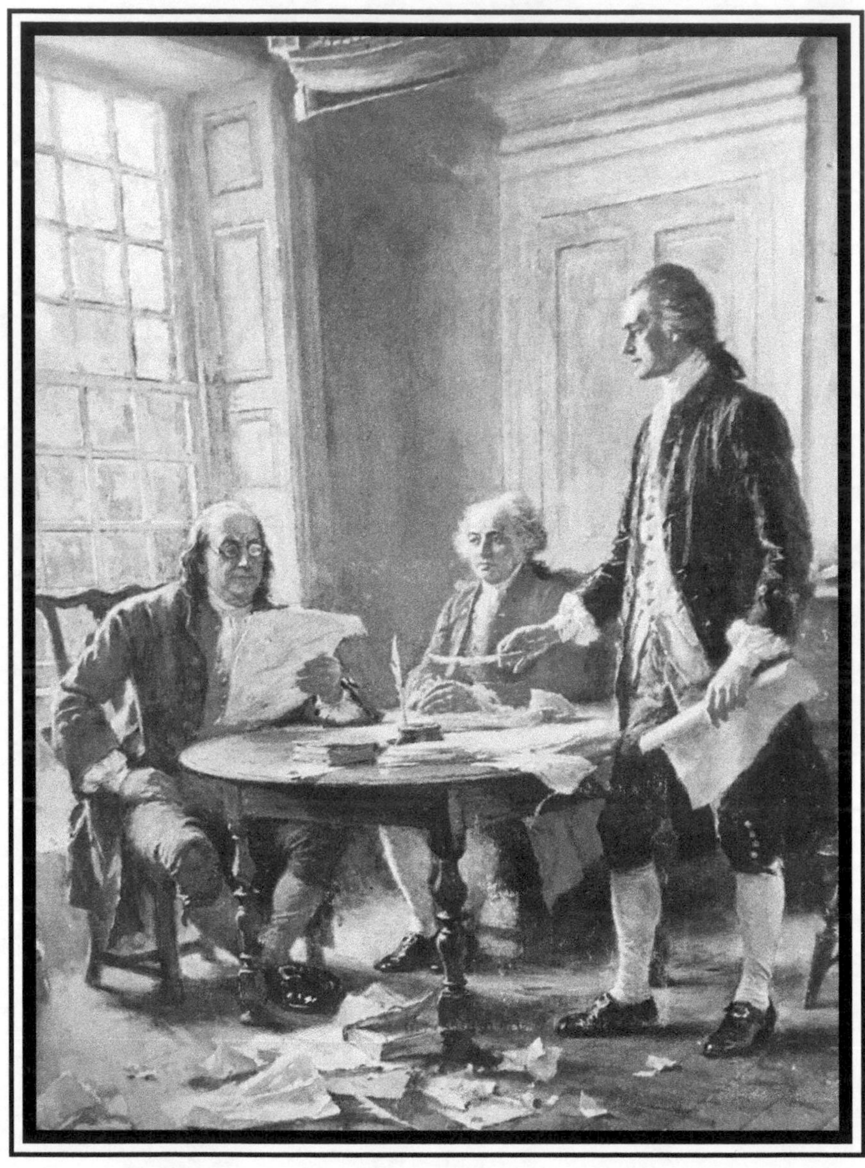

"Drafting the Declaration of Independence" by J.L.G. Ferris. Benjamin Franklin and John Adams go over the text with Thomas Jefferson in Jefferson's rented apartment in Philadelphia. (Courtesy of the Smithsonian Institution)

Brick Tower Press
Manhanset House
Dering Harbor, New York 11965-0342
bricktower@aol.com

Library of Congress Cataloging-in-Publication Data
Nieuwsma, Milton
Inventing America

Includes biographical references and footnotes
ISBN 978-1-899694-90-7, trade paper. ISBN 978-1-899694-91-4, hardcover.

1. PERFORMING ARTS / Television / Guides & Reviews 2. HISTORY / United States / Revolutionary Period (1775-1800) 3. LAW / Constitutional

Nonfiction

First Printing, April 2020

INVENTING America

Conversations with the Founders

Milton J. Nieuwsma

Brick Tower Press
Habent Sua Fata Libelli

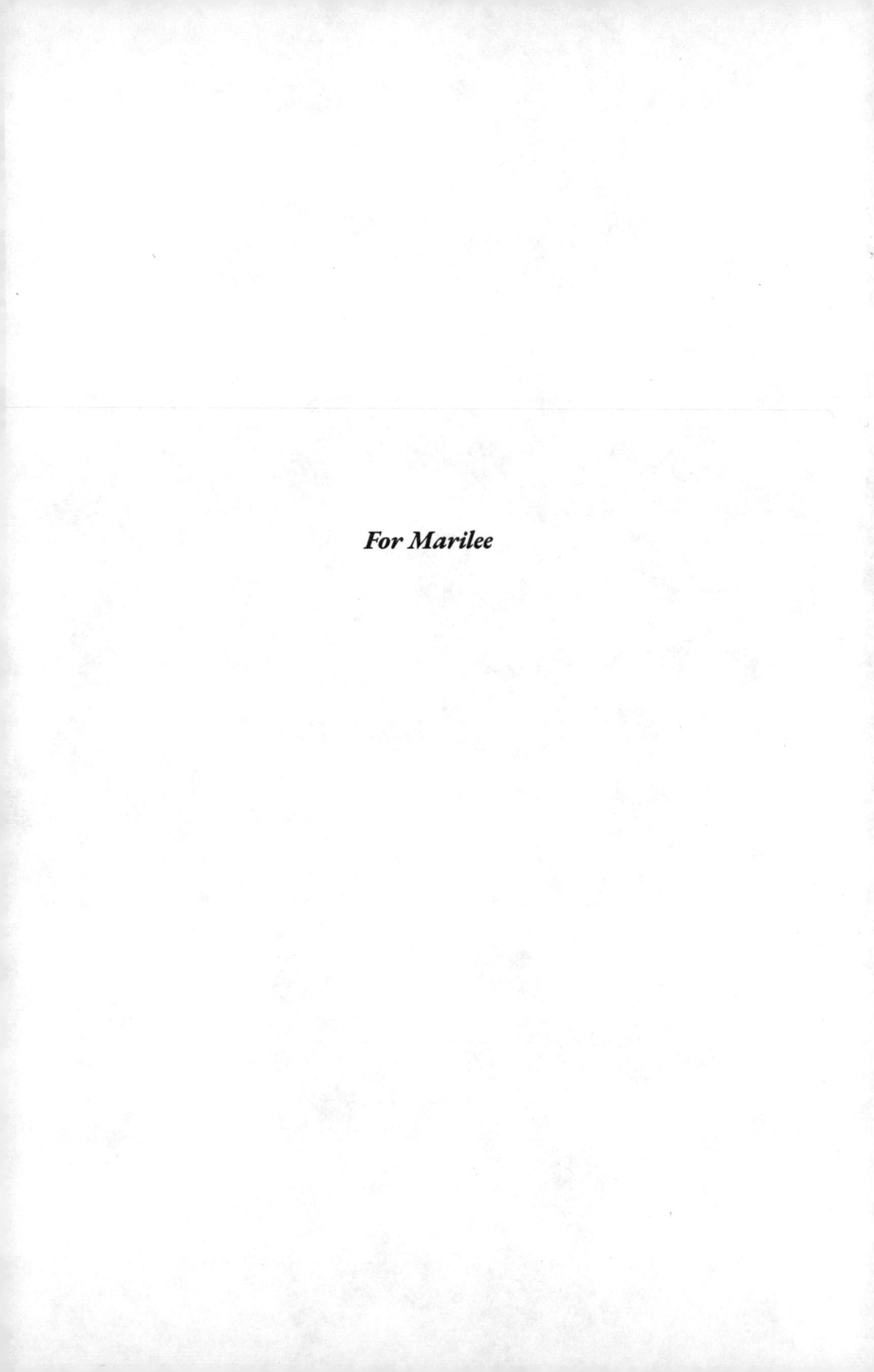

For Marilee

INTRODUCTION

If American college students were tested on their knowledge of U.S. history, the vast majority would flunk. That was the finding of the Roper organization, which in 2012 surveyed graduating seniors at fifty-five of the nation's top-ranked colleges and universities. These were the startling results:

- Three out of five could not identify George Washington as the American general at the battle of Yorktown, the climactic battle of the American Revolution.
- Three out of four could not identify James Madison as the "Father of the Constitution."
- Four out of five could not identify "government of the people, by the people, for the people" as a line from Abraham Lincoln's Gettysburg Address.
- Two out of three could not identify the Constitution as establishing the three divisions of power in the U.S. government.

Yet, when tested on their knowledge of American pop culture, ninety-nine percent knew who the cartoon characters Beavis and Butthead were, and ninety-eight percent identified the rap singer Snoop Dogg.

When our Founding Fathers undertook the great American experiment, they viewed an educated electorate as crucial to its success. But as the Roper survey pointed out, our future leaders are graduating from college with an alarming ignorance of our national heritage, a condition that bodes ill for the future of our republic.

How, then, can we better educate the American public—especially our young people—about who we are? Upon what principles was American democracy founded? And how can we remain true to these principles in a complex and divided world?

To help close this crucial knowledge gap my alma mater, Hope College in Holland, Michigan, in association with WGVU Public Media, began production in 2014 of a three-part public television series, Inventing America: Conversations with the Founders. Blending humor with substance, our mission was to bring our Founding Fathers back to life before a 21st century audience. While we imagined the conversations and presented them in the format of a television talk show, we based them on fact, using the Founders' actual words as much as possible. In the first four years after its premiere, the program reached more than sixteen million viewers.

This book, intended as a companion to the television program, contains the complete scripts for the three episodes along with discussion questions and copies of the Declaration of Independence and Constitution of the United States.

Making a Nation tells the story behind the Declaration of Independence. It features three of the Declaration's signers—Thomas Jefferson, John Adams and Benjamin Franklin—and one delegate to the Second Continental Congress who refused to sign, John Dickinson, revealing the conflict behind this historic event.

Making a Government tells the story behind the Constitutional Convention of 1787, four momentous months that changed the world. James Madison, Alexander Hamilton, Benjamin Franklin, Gouverneur Morris and George Washington discuss the conflicts and compromises that led to creating the world's most enduring republic.

Liberty for All reveals the infighting behind the ratification of the Constitution and how that led to the Bill of Rights. James Madison,

Thomas Jefferson, Alexander Hamilton and Patrick Henry describe how they overcame their differences to create another historic wonder, one that not only defines who we are as Americans but serves as a beacon of freedom to the world.

The scripts are designed for classroom reading and discussion and for live performances, or you may find a quiet place and read them for your own enjoyment. Either way, may you relive our country's formative years as our Founders lived them, see our country's future as they saw it, and come away with a renewed sense of what it means to be American.

MILTON J. NIEUWSMA
Writer and Creator
Inventing America: Conversations with the Founders

AUTHOR'S NOTE

I drew the conversations in this book from letters, diaries, memoirs and other documents left by our Founding Fathers (see Source Notes). As such, I attempted to faithfully convey their words and ideas, not to mention their district personality traits, to a contemporary audience. But where I found the somewhat stilted, ornamental English of the 18th century too awkward to render into everyday speech (try reading a letter of George Washington's out loud!), I endeavored to tune it to 21st century ears.

ACKNOWLEDGMENTS

If you came of age with public television as I did, chances are you saw Steve Allen's Meeting of Minds. The program, which aired on PBS from 1977 to 1981, brought to life famous historical figures in a contemporary-style TV talk show. On one episode you might find Queen Cleopatra extolling her pagan gods to a skeptical Thomas Aquinas; on another, Charles Darwin trying to explain his theory of evolution to Attila the Hun. The program was at once informative, stimulating and entertaining. It made the learning of history fun.

Thanks to Charles Furman, a co-founder of WGVU, the PBS affiliate in Grand Rapids, Michigan, Meeting of Minds became the inspiration for Inventing America. It was Chuck, with whom I had worked on two earlier PBS projects, who came up with the idea of telling America's story the way Steve Allen might have told it: from the point-of-view of our Founding Fathers. But to my great sadness, he did not live to see his idea become a reality.

For that I am in debt to an old and dear friend, Darell Schregardus, who as executive producer had the vision and wherewithal to see the project through to completion; to Marc Baer, professor emeritus of history at Hope College who got his college—my alma mater—to be the venue for it (he doubled as host and producer); to John Tammi, the founder of Hope's acclaimed Summer Repertory Theatre who directed the show, and Hope history professor Fred Johnson, who shared the hosting responsibilities with Marc. For all of us, Inventing America was a labor of love.

I am in debt to the cast and crew for exceeding my expectations for this project. The cast included Bill Barker as Thomas Jefferson, Tom Bengston as Gouverneur Morris, Hal Bidlack as Alexander Hamilton, Sam Goodyear as John Adams, John Douglas Hall as James Madison, John Hamant as Benjamin Franklin, Richard Schumann as Patrick Henry, Rodney TeSlaa as John Dickinson, and Gary Zell as George Washington. The film crew included Phil Lane, director; Zach Liniewski, editor; and Vance Orr, graphic designer. All worked their magic in their own special way.

I am grateful to historians Marc Baer, John Mulder, Gleaves Whitney and the late Richard Beeman for vetting the scripts and keeping me faithful to the facts, and to cast members Barker, Bidlack, Goodyear, Hall, Hamant and Schumann for expanding my insights into the characters they portrayed. All are historians in their own right. Thanks to my publisher, John Colby, for his faith in the idea of a companion book and for making it happen.

I thank the many people in the Hope College administration who backed this project: President John Knapp and his successor, Dennis Voskuil; Patricia Cranmer, Jennifer Fellinger, Greg Olgers, Mary Remenschneider, John Ruiter, Scott Travis, Jim Van Heest, and the Hope College Theatre Department—in particular Perry Landes, Michelle Bombe, Reagan Chesnut, Daina Robbins and Richard Smith. My thanks also to Becky Fry Debowski for her excellent work on the teacher resources for this project.

Finally, I thank my family for all the moral support they have given me—my sons Jonathan and Greg, my daughter Elizabeth, and most of all my wife Marilee. For fifty-six years she has been my light, my love, my rock. It is to her I dedicate this book.

CONTENTS

EPISODE 1

Making a Nation

The Untold Story of
the Declaration of Independence

STAGING NOTE

Episode 1 takes place in the present, but the Founders appear as they would have two or three decades after the Declaration of Independence. The set may suggest the assembly room of the Pennsylvania State House, or it may simply be a table covered in green baize with five Windsor chairs against a neutral backdrop. On the table there is a teapot with four cups and an inkwell with quill.

CAST OF CHARACTERS

JOHN ADAMS (1735-1826). Delegate from Massachusetts. The most outspoken advocate for independence in the Second Continental Congress, he was "obnoxious, suspected and unpopular" by his own admission and was viewed by his colleagues as impetuous, vain, and highly opinionated. Nevertheless, he commanded respect for his integrity and intellect. While deferential to fellow delegates Benjamin Franklin and Thomas Jefferson, he was openly contemptuous of John Dickinson.

BENJAMIN FRANKLIN (1706-1790). Delegate from Pennsylvania. Wise in the ways of courts and empires, he was the most famous man in America. Supported by a cane, his long hair trailing over his shoulders, he personified philosophic tranquility. After spending a decade as the colonies' agent to the Court of St. James, his inclination toward compromise conflicted with his renewed identity as an American. In Congress he served as intermediary (usually without success) between John Adams and John Dickinson.

THOMAS JEFFERSON (1743-1826). Delegate from Virginia. Elected to Congress as a replacement for his mother's cousin, he was an unknown when he arrived in Philadelphia. Soft-spoken and modest, he was neither an effective speaker nor a political heavyweight. Throughout his tenure in Congress, it was his wish to return home and tend to his ailing wife. Yet time and circumstances conspired to secure his place in history as the author of the Declaration of Independence.

JOHN DICKINSON (1732-1808). Delegate from Pennsylvania. The opposite of John Adams in personality and temperament and his chief rival in Congress, the "farmer from Pennsylvania" sought to the end to mend fences with the Mother Country. Adams called him a "piddling genius." More charitable colleagues thought of him as well-meaning if wrong-headed. No matter. The unfortunate Mr. Dickinson, by refusing to sign the Declaration of Independence, was to find himself on the wrong side of history.

EPISODE 1

Making a Nation

MODERATOR: Welcome to *Inventing America*. When the American colonies declared their independence from Great Britain, they not only defied the most powerful nation on earth, they set into motion the founding of the first modern republic. What happened in the summer of 1776 was nothing short of a miracle. But how long would it last? Tonight, we meet four distinguished delegates to the Second Continental Congress in Philadelphia. They're going to tell us, in their own words, about the miracle they pulled off. Their story is the untold story of the Declaration of Independence. But it's our story, too.

Let's go back to the Pennsylvania State House in Philadelphia. Today we call it Independence Hall. It's where fifty-six delegates from thirteen British colonies in North America came to thrash out what to do about taxes the British Parliament had imposed on the colonies, taxes the colonies deemed unfair because they had no voice in the matter. As British subjects an ocean away from the seat of power, they had nobody to represent them in Parliament. So they came together after Lord North, the British Prime Minister, showed he meant business.

And how did he do that? By sending British troops to confront American militia in Concord, Massachusetts. Across the Concord River, in neighboring Lexington, a shot rang out on the morning of April 19, 1775. Nobody knew who fired it, but it started a revolution that changed the world.

Each of our guests tonight played a critical role in that event. Our first guest is a lawyer by profession but a farmer at heart who sprang to prominence—perhaps notoriety is a better word—when he successfully defended British redcoats for their role in the Boston Massacre, one of the events that led to the Revolution. Later he went on to head the new republic. Would you please welcome from the State of Massachusetts the second president of the United States, Mr. John Adams. *(Adams enters and seats himself.)*

MODERATOR: It's a pleasure to have you on the program, Mr. President.

ADAMS: Thank you.

MODERATOR: Sir, in the 21st century we think of you as the most outspoken champion of American independence. You gave more speeches, took part in more debates than even Patrick Henry. Yet early in your career you defended a number of redcoats charged with murder after the Boston Massacre. Why?

ADAMS: That's correct. But before I answer that I want to clarify something. You said the American Revolution started when the first shot was fired at Lexington. It actually started much earlier than that, and it didn't start with gunpowder. It started with molasses.

MODERATOR: Molasses?

ADAMS: Yes, molasses. It started when Parliament passed the Molasses Act in 1733—ten years before my colleague from Virginia, Mr. Jefferson—say, isn't he joining us?

MODERATOR: He will a bit later.

ADAMS: Well, it started ten years before he was born. The law forbade the colonies from importing sugar from outside the British Empire, and lord knows how we Americans love sugar. When James Otis, a lawyer colleague in Boston, fought it in a British court and lost, it was then and there the child Independence was born.

MODERATOR: I stand corrected. You were around then, I wasn't.

ADAMS: I was, sir, but a gleam in my father's eye in 1733, but I do know my history.

MODERATOR: Well, I'm sure of that.

ADAMS: Now as to why I defended the redcoats. The Boston Massacre as you call it—I think of it as the Boston riot because there was fault on both sides—it happened because the British had sent army troops to Boston to enforce the Townshend Acts which Parliament had passed in 1767.

MODERATOR: Tell me about the Townshend Acts.

ADAMS: They were named for Charles Townshend, the Chancellor of the Exchequer, who came up with the idea, which turned out not to be a very good one. Partly their purpose was to force the colonies to comply with the Navigation Acts which regulated trade. But mostly—and this is what really got the Americans' dander up—it was a veiled attempt by Parliament to buy the allegiance of colonial governors by paying their salaries.

MODERATOR: How did Parliament propose to do that?

ADAMS: By taxing the colonies.

MODERATOR: So let me get this straight. Parliament was buying their loyalty with ransom money from the colonies.

ADAMS: Precisely. Not only did that infringe on the colonies' right to govern themselves, but it established the precedent that Parliament had the right to tax them.

MODERATOR: But hadn't the Stamp Act already done that?

ADAMS: Ah, the Stamp Act, 1765. There the dispute wasn't just about taxation. It was about whether Parliament had any authority at all in the colonies. The law proved so unpopular that Parliament repealed it a year later.

MODERATOR: So why was Parliament taxing the colonies in the first place?

ADAMS: To pay for the Seven Years' War.

MODERATOR: You mean the French and Indian War.

ADAMS: Well, that was what the Americans called it because over here it had to do with the British taking land occupied by the French and the Indians. But it really had to do with the British expanding their empire around the world. You could really call it the first world war.

MODERTATOR: What time frame are you talking about?

ADAMS: 1756 TO 1763, seven years. By the time the British finished their campaign their empire took in a quarter of the world's population, from India and the Pacific to coastal Africa and most of North America. Think of it, one-fourth of the human race! And those victories cost a lot of money, not to mention the cost of policing all the new land they acquired. Hence the taxes.

MODERATOR: Even though the Americans had nothing to do it.

ADAMS: Well, George Washington of Virginia served as a colonel under a British commander against the French and Indians, but he wasn't very good. He never won a battle.

MODERATOR: So back to the Boston Massacre.

ADAMS *(correcting the moderator):* The Boston riot. Well, yes. They were a motley rabble of saucy boys, Negroes and mulattos, Irish teagues and outlandish jack tars. They taunted the British soldiers to fire at them, which they did. Three civilians were killed on the spot and two died later. Eight soldiers were tried for murder. I argued that they had the right to defend themselves because their lives were in danger. The jury acquitted all eight.

MODERATOR: Your defending them must have come at some personal cost.

ADAMS: It did. I devoted myself to endless labor and anxiety, if not to infamy and death, out of a sense of duty. After all, they had the right to a fair trial. When I expressed my apprehension to Mrs. Adams she burst into tears because she was sensible of the danger to her and our children as well as to me. But, bless her heart, she said I had done as I ought and placed her trust in Providence.

MODERATOR: So the Boston Massacre—

ADAMS: —the Boston riot.

MODERATOR: So the Boston riot took place in 1770, five years before Lexington and Concord. What happened after that?

ADAMS: Even though I had won the soldiers' acquittal, depictions of the riot found their way through the colonies, including an engraving by a Boston silversmith named Paul Revere. After that, relations between England and the Massachusetts colony went into freefall. As the British stepped up their military presence to enforce compliance with all their new laws and taxes, we stepped up our resistance. The tax on tea was the last straw. Sam Adams, a cousin of mine, rounded up a group of men, had them dress up as Indians, and they raided three merchant ships in Boston Harbor, ships owned by the British East India Company. They dumped—what did he tell me—342 chests of tea into the harbor. That's about £10,000 worth.

MODERATOR: Who did you say rounded up the men?

ADAMS: My cousin, Samuel Adams.

MODERATOR: It wasn't beer they threw into the harbor?

ADAMS: What are you talking about?

MODERATOR: Never mind. Tell me about your cousin.

ADAMS: Oh, well, Sam was a maltster but never ran a brewery if that's what you're thinking. In fact, he was a terrible businessman. I remember when his father loaned him £1,000 so he could start his own business. Sam loaned half to a friend who never paid it back. The other half he frittered away. After that his father made him a partner in the family's malt house, which produced malt for making beer, but Sam was never a brewmeister. Indeed, he failed at every business venture he tried. But he was an effective polemist for the American cause, a true patriot I must say, and I had the pleasure of serving with him in the Continental Congress.

MODERATOR: So he was the guy behind the tea party.

ADAMS: The tea party?

MODERATOR: Yes, the Boston Tea Party.

ADAMS: Good lord! Is that what you call it now? How history puts labels on things!

MODERATOR: Speaking of tea, would you care for some?

ADAMS *(suspiciously)*: It isn't taxed is it?

MODERATOR *(pouring tea):* Not anymore, not here anyway.

ADAMS: Where did it come from?

MODERATOR *(pauses, looks up)*: Trader Joe's.

ADAMS *(bewildered)*: Thank you. *(Drinks)*

MODERATOR *(to the audience)*: While John Adams and his cousin Samuel and their fellow patriots were protesting British taxes and throwing tea into Boston Harbor, our next guest was in London pleading the American cause. We might think of him as the first American lobbyist. But he was much more than that. He was a printer, pamphleteer, scientist, inventor, statesman, advice-giver. He was Leonardo de Vinci and Dear Abby all wrapped into one. Today we think of him as the quintessential American. Ladies and gentlemen, please welcome Dr. Benjamin Franklin. *(Franklin enters with a cane, bows, and seats himself.)*

MODERATOR: It's an honor to have you on the program, sir. Would you like some tea?

FRANKLIN: Don't mind if I do. Thank you. By the way, who is Dear Abby?

MODERATOR *(pours tea)*: She writes an advice column.

FRANKLIN: Well, I used to do that too, you know. In fact, I devoted a whole magazine to giving people advice. I called it *Poor Richard's Almanack.* I figured since I had been around so long, I had lots of advice to give.

MODERATOR: I'm sure it was very good advice.

FRANKLIN: Would you like to hear some? "A stitch in time saves nine."

MODERATOR: Thank you, sir.

FRANKLIN: "A penny saved is a penny earned."

MODERATOR: Very good, sir.

FRANKLIN: "An apple a day keeps the doctor away."

MODERATOR: Very good, sir, thank you.

FRANKLIN: "Fish and visitors stink in three days."

MODERATOR: Thank you, sir. Could we move on?

FRANKLIN *(sighs)*: As you wish.

MODERATOR: Mr. Adams was just filling me in on what happened while you were away in London. Did you know about all those things like the tea party and the Boston Massacre—?

ADAMS *(interrupting)*: —the Boston riot.

FRANKLIN: I did of course, but it took anywhere from four to six weeks to get the news depending on the wind.

MODERATOR: The wind?

FRANKLIN: Yes, over the Atlantic. That's how long it took ships to cross. I didn't learn about Lexington until a month after it happened. Time delays were the hobgoblin of diplomacy. It isn't that way anymore I suppose.

MODERATOR: Not anymore, but I'm not sure that's an advantage.

FRANKLIN: I spent long stretches of time in London because the voyages were long and difficult, especially for someone of my years, and sometimes the ships didn't make it.

MODERATOR: How long was your last stay in London?

FRANKLIN: Ten years, from 1765—just in time to see the Stamp Act passed—to May of '75. Before that I had spent eight years there.

MODERATOR: Did you have your family with you?

FRANKLIN: Just my son, William, in the early years. My wife, Deborah, refused to go. She was more terrified of the sea than I was.

MODERATOR: So the last time you were there you didn't see your wife for ten years.

FRANKLIN: That's right. Technically it was nine because she died in '74.

MODERATOR: I take it you didn't make it back for her funeral.

FRANKLIN *(wiping his eyes):* I still have a verse I wrote to her. May I read it? *(Reaches into his vest for a piece of paper.)*

MODERATOR: Please do.

FRANKLIN *(reads):*

Not a Word of her Face, her Shape, or her Eyes,
Of Flames or of Darts shall you hear?
Though' Beauty I admire 'tis Virtue I prize,
That fades not in seventy Years.

(Returns the paper to his vest.) She died of a stroke.

ADAMS: I'm sorry, Ben. But I don't recall that you ever mentioned her.

FRANKLIN: I didn't, because we were never legally married. She was married to somebody else. Her husband had taken her dowry and fled to Barbados to avoid debtors' prison and was never heard from again. She couldn't legally marry me because of bigamy laws. So we lived together under common law and she agreed to raise my illegitimate son.

ADAMS: That would be William.

FRANKLIN: Yes, William. What a fine boy he was...smart... industrious...affectionate. He stood with me when I did my electricity experiment with the kite.

MODERATOR: Sir, if I may, I would like to ask you about the Stamp Act that Parliament passed in 1765.

FRANKLIN: Well, yes. I had been home for just a year when the Pennsylvania Assembly elected me as their speaker. But five months later I was relieved of that responsibility.

MODERATOR: How come?

FRANKLIN: When William Penn founded the colony in 1682 he had it chartered under his name by the British Crown. That gave his descendents veto power over any laws we made. When I came out in opposition to their veto power, they had me replaced.

MODERATOR: That doesn't sound very democratic—

FRANKLIN: —which is why I went back to England: It was to persuade Parliament to end the Penn family's hold on the colony. No sooner had I gotten back Parliament passed the Stamp Act.

MODERATOR: Just what was the Stamp Act?

FRANKLIN: It was a tax imposed on the colonies to help pay for

British troops who remained after the French and Indian War. All printed materials had to have a British stamp—legal documents, newspapers, magazines, playing cards, you name it. And the stamp had to be purchased with British currency. I arrived too late to talk Parliament out of it.

ADAMS *(to Franklin):* But that didn't stop you, Ben, from appointing a friend of yours—what was his name?—John Hughes—to collect the stamp tax in Pennsylvania. Don't you remember that a mob tried to tear your house down in protest?

FRANKLIN: I regret that I ever had anything to do with the stamp tax. Though I spoke in opposition to it later and got Parliament to repeal it, I had no idea how vehement the sentiment in America was against it.

ADAMS: You were in England too long, Ben. You were out of touch.

FRANKLIN *(to the moderator):* It wasn't until Parliament passed the Coercive Acts in retaliation for what you call the Boston Tea Party that I began to realize the futility of my mission in London. So in 1775 I came home. When I arrived in Philadelphia I learned about the battle at Lexington and Concord. I knew then and there that no colony could act alone. We had to act as one—*e pluribus unum.*

ADAMS: Twelve of the colonies had already sent representatives to a General Congress in Philadelphia to discuss what to do in response to the Coercive Acts. That was in the fall of '74 when we met at Carpenters' Hall. We called for a boycott of British imports and petitioned the King for a redress of our grievances. When our appeal fell on deaf ears, we called for a Second General Congress. That one convened in Philadelphia on May 10, 1775. *(Turns to Franklin.)* Ben, hadn't you just returned from England?—

FRANKLIN: —five days before—

ADAMS: —and you were added to the Pennsylvania delegation.

FRANKLIN: The day after I got off the ship in Philadelphia. That's correct.

ADAMS *(to the moderator)*: Then a month later a young man arrived from Virginia to take his seat. He couldn't have been much over thirty at the time. His name was Thomas Jefferson. He brought with him a reputation for literature and science and a happy talent for composition. Everyone was talking about a paper he had written called *A Summary View of the Rights of British America*. That was the first time I had heard of him. Why he arrived so late I don't remember.

MODERATOR: Well, let's ask him. *(Turns to the audience.)* Our next guest actually was thirty-two when he took his seat in the Second Continental Congress. He, too, went on to bigger and better things. But when he arrived in Philadelphia the summer of 1775, nobody outside his colony knew much about him. Would you welcome, please, from the state of Virginia, the third president of the United States, Mr. Thomas Jefferson. *(Jefferson enters with a violin, nods, and sits down beside Franklin.)* Welcome, Mr. President. It's a pleasure to have you on the program.

JEFFERSON: Indeed, the pleasure is mine.

MODERATOR: I see you have a violin with you.

JEFFERSON: It's the reason I arrived late at the Continental Congress—at least one of the reasons.

MODERATOR: How so?

JEFFERSON: This violin belonged to my cousin, John Randolph. On my way to Philadelphia from Monticello, my home near Charlottesville, I stopped over in Williamsburg to bid him farewell.

MODERATOR: I don't understand.

JEFFERSON: Many years ago, when we were but young law students in Williamsburg, we played the violin together at the Governor's Palace. This was his violin, hand-made in Cremona, Italy, 1660. See the date? *(Passes the violin to Franklin who squints through the opening)* I made an agreement with John that if I died first he would inherit my books; if he died first I would inherit his violin. It was all very official—signed and sealed in the General Court in Williamsburg. George Wythe, my law teacher, and Patrick Henry were the witnesses. Then the war broke out at

Lexington. John chose to side with England. Before he set sail "for home" as he put it, he gave me his violin.

ADAMS *(notices Franklin wiping his eyes):* Are you all right, Ben? *(Jefferson takes the violin from Franklin and places it on the table.)*

JEFFERSON *(solicitously)*: Sir, was it something I said?

FRANKLIN *(shaking his head):* No, no, I'm fine. It's just that your story makes me think of William.

MODERATOR: Your son?

FRANKLIN *(removes a handkerchief from his vest and wipes his eyes)*: Yes, my son William. I put everything I had into raising him. When so many people ridiculed my scientific experiments, it was William who stood beside me when I raised my kite into the clouds to prove that lightening was electricity. I knew how proud he was of me at that moment. After he grew up, I was just as proud of him when George III appointed him the royal governor of New Jersey. On my voyage back from England I wrote him the longest letter I had ever written—ninety-seven pages. I poured my heart out. I told him how I tried to get Parliament to repeal the Tea Act—how all my overtures for reconciliation had failed and why I thought he should resign his appointment. Then when I got off the ship, I heard the news from Lexington.

MODERATOR: Did he ever answer your letter?

FRANKLIN *(pauses, wipes his eyes again):* His answer was to mount an assault against the patriots. Nothing ever hurt me so much as to find myself deserted in my old age by my only son. Not only deserted but to find him taking up arms against me in a cause wherein my life, my fortune, my sacred honor were all at stake.

JEFFERSON *(places his hand over Franklin's arm)*: I'm sorry, sir.

ADAMS: I'm sorry too, Ben. (*Turns to the moderator.)* But you know, defections like Dr. Franklin's son and Mr. Jefferson's cousin were not at all unusual. Our troubles with England split a lot of families apart. You were either a loyalist or a patriot or you didn't give a damn.

JEFFERSON *(to the moderator)*: In fact, it was John Randolph's brother, Payton Randolph, whose seat I inherited in the Continental Congress.

MODERATOR: Is that so?

JEFFERSON: And that's the other reason I came late.

MODERATOR: Can you explain?

JEFFERSON: Payton Randolph—my mother's cousin to be more precise—was the speaker of the Virginia House of Burgesses—

ADAMS: —and the first president of the Continental Congress.

JEFFERSON: That's correct, and he needed somebody to take his place at Virginia's table in case he got called back to Williamsburg. So he nominated me. It happened at St. John's Church in Richmond where the burgesses met in convention to decide how far to pursue the conflict with England. All the talk was about Patrick Henry's speech—"Give me liberty or give me death." Where he got that torrent of language from I don't know because he was the laziest man for reading I ever knew—all tongue, no head. But no matter, on the last day of the convention I was elected an alternate delegate for Payton Randolph. Nobody took much notice.

MODERATOR: So that's how you came into the Continental Congress.

JEFFERSON: As an afterthought. You might say I came through the back door.

ADAMS: Well, Tom, you were only how old when you were elected?

JEFFERSON: Thirty-one. *(To the moderator)* But please don't misunderstand. *How* I came was not the issue. That I came at all was the issue. It wasn't my choice to come. I was needed at home. My wife was ill. So was my younger daughter.

MODERATOR: The separation must have been difficult.

JEFFERSON: All the while I was anxious for word about my wife who stayed behind in Virginia. *(Pauses)* As for my daughter, Jane, she died at 18 months. *(Adams and Franklin mumble their condolences.)*

MODERATOR *(to Jefferson)*: Yet you did come, sir, and what a difference that made. It's impossible today to imagine our country without the *Declaration of Independence.* May I ask you how it came into being?

JEFFERSON: Before the Virginia convention met in Williamsburg to pick delegates to the first General Congress, I had some time to myself at Monticello. So I buried myself in my study and reflected on our colonies' relationship with England and the abuses that had taken place. I put my thoughts in writing along with draft instructions for the delegates to Philadelphia.

ADAMS *(to the moderator):* That was the paper I mentioned, *A Summary View of the Rights of British America.*

JEFFERSON: But that wasn't the title I had given it, nor had I given permission to have it printed.

MODERATOR *(holds up Jefferson's paper):* I have a copy of it here. So how did it come to be printed?

JEFFERSON: I was on my way to Williamsburg, on horseback, and had it tucked in my saddlebag when I fell ill and had to turn back. From my bed I wrote out two copies by hand and sent one by courier to Mr. Henry and one to Mr. Randolph to present at the convention. Mr. Henry confessed to me later that he never read his copy. Mr. Randolph had not only read his copy but had it printed in Williamsburg.

MODERATOR: What was the gist of your paper?

JEFFERSON: I argued that our emigration from England to North America had given England no more rights over us than the emigrations of the Danes and Saxons to England had given *their* mother country.

MODERATOR: But weren't the Americans British subjects and therefore subject to the laws of Parliament?

JEFFERSON: Ah, that was the rub. I argued that because the Americans had submitted *voluntarily* to Parliament's authority, we could, if we chose to do so, release ourselves from that authority. What was freely given could freely be taken away.

MODERATOR: As the Bible says, "The Lord giveth, the Lord taketh away."

JEFFERSON: In this case it was the Americans. I questioned whether Parliament had any right to impose the stamp tax and the Townshend duties. I questioned whether it had any right to close the Port of Boston. Indeed, could it justify under any written treaty or simply the nature of things reducing that city to beggary because of the actions of a few who were *already* subject to the laws of their own colony?

MODERATOR: Sir, may I prevail on you to read a few passages? *(Hands Jefferson his copy and points to an open page)* Please, starting right here if you don't mind.

JEFFERSON *(gives the moderator a startled glance and reads):* "Scarcely have our minds been able to emerge from the astonishments into which one stroke of parliamentary thunder has involved us, before another more heavy and alarming is fallen on us. Single acts of tyranny may be ascribed to the accidental opinion of a day, but a series of oppressions, begun at a distinguished period and pursued unalterably through every stage of ministers, too plainly prove a deliberate, systematical plan of reducing us to slavery." *(Adams is nodding his head; Franklin is rocking back and forth on his cane, his eyes closed.)* Do you want me to continue?

MODERATOR: Please do.

JEFFERSON *(resumes reading)*: "A free people claim their rights as derived from the laws of nature, not as the gift of their chief magistrate.... Can His Majesty thus put down all laws under his feet? Can he erect a power superior to himself? He has done it indeed by force; but let him remember that force cannot give right.... Kings are the servants, not the proprietors of the people....Let not the name of George the Third be a blot on the page of history." *(Adams thumps the table while Franklin looks on, slightly agitated.)*

MODERATOR *(to Jefferson)*: You wrote this when?

JEFFERSON: In 1774, before the Virginia convention met in Williamsburg.

MODERATOR: And the purpose of that convention was to elect delegates to the General Congress in Philadelphia.

JEFFERSON: That's correct.

MODERATOR: So what happened to your paper at the Virginia convention?

JEFFERSON *(slaps his paper down on the table)*: It died on the table. Payton Randolph told me that tamer sentiments were preferred.

MODERATOR: But the printed version found its way to Philadelphia—

FRANKLIN: —and to London, where it procured Mr. Jefferson the honor of being listed in a bill of attainder.

MODERATOR: A bill of attainder?

FRANKLIN: A criminal indictment by Parliament. I tried to prevent that too but couldn't. It made Mr. Jefferson a fugitive from justice.

MODERATOR: And if he'd been caught?

FRANKLIN: He would have been hanged for treason.

ADAMS: But that was true of all of us, Ben.

FRANKLIN: Which is why I said, "We must all hang together, or most assuredly we will all hang separately." Remember?

MODERATOR: Well put, Dr. Franklin. So let's talk about the Second Continental Congress. Mr. Jefferson, you said you arrived late.

JEFFERSON: Yes, it wasn't until Mr. Randolph was called back to Williamsburg to preside over the House of Burgesses that I came to replace him. It was the 21st of June, 1775, two months after Lexington. When I arrived, I learned that George Washington, a fellow delegate from Virginia, had also vacated his seat.

MODERATOR: Why so?

JEFFERSON: To take command of the Continental Army.

ADAMS: Well, I'm the one to blame for that.

MODERATOR: Oh?

ADAMS: I was the one who nominated him. It was to keep John Hancock from becoming the commander-in-chief. You see, it was

Hancock, not Washington, who really wanted the job and expected it. I can see him now sitting in the President's Chair—he had taken Mr. Randolph's place. Hancock listened with visible pleasure while I was making my nominating speech, and when I came around to describing Washington as my choice, I never saw a more sudden change of countenance. Ha! Ha! His jaw dropped a mile!

MODERATOR *(perplexed):* But the British were encamped in Boston, Hancock's home town. Why did you nominate Washington instead of Hancock?

ADAMS: Partly to keep his vanity in check. I have never known anyone to equal him on that score.

FRANKLIN: You should talk, John.

ADAMS: I admit to having my share of vanity, Ben. But Hancock had the most obstinate case I ever saw. Did you ever notice how he signs his name? *(Gestures broadly)* JOHN HANCOCK. *(Turns to the moderator)* But the main reason I nominated Washington was that he was a Southerner. We Bostonians—all of us from Massachusetts in fact—were a highly suspect lot. Nobody from the middle colonies trusted us except Dr. Franklin.

MODERATOR: What about Mr. Dickinson.

ADAMS: John Dickinson? Surely you jest!

MODERATOR: Wasn't it Mr. Dickinson who called attention to the folly of the Townshend duties in his *Letters from a Pennsylvania Farmer*?

ADAMS: But *then* what did he do? After Lexington he drew up an *Olive Branch Petition* in an attempt to appease the king. Imagine that! It embarrassed every exertion we made in the Congress. It was an act of imbecility, the work of a piddling genius!

FRANKLIN: Now, John, calm down. We can't all have the same views on the same subject at the same time. Besides, I always found Mr. Dickinson to be a man of sound character. I'm sure he had his reasons.

MODERATOR: Well, let's find out what his reasons were.

ADAMS: What are you talking about?

MODERATOR: Let's have Mr. Dickinson speak for himself.

ADAMS: Good lord! You didn't invite *him* to sit at this table, did you?

MODERATOR: We still have an empty chair. Ladies and gentlemen, please welcome the Farmer from Pennsylvania, Mr. John Dickinson. *(Dickinson enters. Everyone but John Adams rises to greet him.)* Thank you, sir, for joining us.

DICKINSON: Thank you for inviting me. (*Sits down.)*

MODERATOR: It had to take some courage for you to accept my invitation knowing Mr. Adams would be here. Would you like some tea?

DICKINSON: Yes, I would. Thank you. *(The moderator pours him a cup of tea. Dickinson takes a sip and frowns.)* It's cold.

ADAMS: Good! *(Franklin and Jefferson glare at him.)*

MODERATOR: My apologies, sir. I wonder if you would tell us about your *Letters from a Pennsylvania Farmer,* which put you at the forefront of the conflict with England at the beginning and then why you pulled back later.

DICKINSON: Thank you for giving me the opportunity. After Parliament passed the Townshend Acts in 1767 I wrote a series of letters for one of Dr. Franklin's newspapers, the *Pennsylvania Gazette,* in which I argued that the taxes Parliament imposed on the colonies were unconstitutional and contrary to natural law. I argued that the right to levy taxes was the sole prerogative of the colonial assemblies. But I supported Parliament's right to enact regulatory duties on trade within the British Empire.

FRANKLIN *(to the moderator):* Mr. Dickinson's letters expressed the American sentiments of the time, which is why I instructed the *Gazette* to publish them. Later other newspapers around the colonies followed suit.

DICKINSON: After I came into the Continental Congress—by then our relations with the Mother Country had greatly worsened—I co-authored with Mr. Jefferson a *Declaration of the Causes of Taking Up Arms* in which I affirmed our resolve to die as free men rather than live as slaves.

FRANKLIN: That too echoed the sentiment of the time.

ADAMS: But then, Mr. Dickinson, you undid all that with your *Olive Branch Petition*. Your timing couldn't have been worse! Did you think the Ministry and Parliament would relent after hearing of the battle at Lexington? What did you expect from them other than deceit and hostility and fire and sword? All your petition did was to cause the king to declare the colonies in rebellion. What on earth possessed you to write it?

DICKINSON: I don't know if you or anyone else here, except Dr. Franklin perhaps, knows what it means to be a Quaker. *(Rises, begins pacing.)* We're opposed to war as much as we are to slavery. But for me it was more than that. *(To Jefferson)* You, sir, had a cousin to deal with, *(turning to Franklin)* and you, sir, had your son; I can't imagine how painful your falling out with him must have been. But, gentlemen, I didn't have just one person in my family to deal with but the entire Quaker establishment in Philadelphia. They never ceased from intimidating my mother and my dear wife who in turn begged me to hold back. *(To Adams)* Do you know what my mother said? She said, "Johnny, if you continue the course you're on, you will be hanged, your estate will be confiscated, you will leave your excellent wife a widow and your charming children orphans and beggars." Wouldn't that give you pause?

ADAMS *(breaking the silence)*: Well, if I'd had such a mother and such a wife, I believe I would have shot myself!

DICKINSON *(insulted)*: I beg your leave, gentlemen. *(Exits.)*

MODERATOR: Well, that was unfortunate. I hope we may persuade Mr. Dickinson to come back.

ADAMS *(sighs)*: I suppose I should apologize to him. *(Follows Dickinson off stage.)*

MODERATOR: Well, that leaves just the three of us for the moment. *(To Jefferson)* Sir, Mr. Dickinson said the taxes that Parliament imposed on the colonies were contrary to natural law. I'm curious about that point since you made similar references in your writings. What did you mean by natural law?

JEFFERSON: Natural law refers to the use of reason to analyze human nature and deduce rules of human behavior. Natural law is distinct from common law in that it views certain rights as inherent and God-given. Common law—man-made law—is the legal tradition that derives from it. Over the years theories about natural law have exercised a profound influence on English common law. Those theories go as far back as Aristotle.

MODERATOR: Aristotle, hmm. What did *he* say about natural law?

JEFFERSON: Aristotle said there was an unchangeable natural law that applied to the human race as well as to the universe. He said that man had a natural inclination to be just. In the 13th century Saint Thomas Aquinas took that a step further and said that man had a natural inclination to the *good*, according to the rational nature that was inherent in him, and that he had a natural inclination to know the truth about God and to live in harmony with the world.

FRANKLIN: Speaking as a scientist, I say Aristotle hit the nail on the head. He was two thousand years ahead of his time. Much later, in the 1680s, Sir Isaac Newton set out to prove that everything that happened in the physical universe—all the movements of the stars and planets—happened in harmony. He said there was a cause-and-effect relationship in every physical movement, that for every action there was an equal and opposite reaction. He maintained that the universe itself was subject to rational inquiry.

JEFFERSON: Then John Locke, the British political philosopher and a contemporary of Newton's, took Newton's theory beyond the physical realm and said, in effect: as natural law governs movements of the universe, so does natural law govern *human* relationships. And what is the role of government but to preserve those relationships of harmony, of balance, and justice?

MODERATOR: I can imagine the impact those ideas had on the colonies when Parliament imposed all those taxes and then sent the troops over to enforce them.

JEFFERSON: The attack on Lexington wasn't just an attack on Lexington. It wasn't just an attack on the colonies. It was an attack on all mankind. Those were the ideas I tried to incorporate in the *Declaration of Independence.*

MODERATOR: I was hoping we would get around to that. Today the *Declaration of Independence* is the thing for which you are most remembered. Did anyone in July of 1776 know that you had written it?

JEFFERSON: Nobody outside the Continental Congress.

MODERATOR: How were you picked to write it?

JEFFERSON: Perhaps Mr. Adams should tell you, but since he isn't here—

FRANKLIN: Excuse me. May I?

MODERATOR: Dr. Franklin, sir.

FRANKLIN: Five of us were chosen to serve on a committee to draw up the document. Help me, Mr. Jefferson, because my memory is a bit fuzzy—

JEFFERSON: Mr. Sherman of Connecticut, Mr. Livingston of New York—

FRANKLIN: That's right.

JEFFERSON: —you, Mr. Adams—

FRANKLIN *(struggling to recall)*: —yes, yes—

JEFFERSON: —and me!

FRANKLIN: That's right. There were five—

JEFFERSON: —two from New England, two from the middle colonies, and one from the south.

FRANKLIN: Yes, I do recall now. I remember having an attack of the gout—

JEFFERSON: —which is why you ruled yourself out, or you would have been the one to write it.

MODERATOR: What about Sherman and Livingston?

JEFFERSON: They were put on the committee for geographical, not literary, reasons.

MODERATOR: So the choice came down to you and Mr. Adams.

JEFFERSON: That's correct. *(Adams enters and resumes his place at the table.)*

ADAMS: Well, I apologized, but Mr. Dickinson said he needed a few minutes to regain his composure. I suspect he'll be back.

MODERATOR: Thank you, sir. We were just talking about how the committee in charge of the *Declaration of Independence* was appointed and how the choice of who should write it came down to you and Mr. Jefferson.

ADAMS: Ah, yes. As I said, Mr. Jefferson brought to the Congress a reputation for literature and a happy talent for composition. Writings of his were handed about, remarkable for their felicity of expression. Although a silent member of Congress—the whole time I sat with him I never heard him utter three sentences together—he was so prompt and explicit and decisive in committees and in conversation that he seized upon my heart. The committee you spoke of met, and then appointed Mr. Jefferson and me to make the draft. Mr. Jefferson proposed to me that I write it, but I refused. "Why will you not?" he asked. "Reasons enough," I said. "What can be your reasons?" And I replied, "Reason first, you're a Virginian, and a Virginian ought to appear at the head of this business. Reason second, I am obnoxious, suspected and unpopular."

FRANKLIN *(chuckling)*: You said it, John, not I.

ADAMS *(ignoring Franklin)*: "You are very much otherwise," I said. "Reason third, you write ten times better than I can." And then Mr. Jefferson said—well, I'll let him finish the story.

JEFFERSON: I said, "Very well, sir, if you're decided, I will do as well as I can."

ADAMS: Meanwhile, a motion was on the floor calling for independence. It had been introduced by another delegate from Virginia, Richard Henry Lee.

FRANKLIN *(rolling out a newspaper):* Here it is, in the *Pennsylvania Gazette*: "Friday, June 7—Resolved, that these united colonies are and of right ought to be free and independent states, that they are absolved from all allegiance to the British crown, and that all connection between them and the State of Great Britain is, and ought to be, totally dissolved."

ADAMS: Let's not forget the role Thomas Paine played in getting us to this point.

MODERATOR: The author of *Common Sense.*

ADAMS: Right. It had just come out. No resolution of the Congress, no paper written by Mr. Jefferson or anybody else, did more to turn the tide of public opinion in favor of independence than Mr. Paine's little pamphlet. His message spread through the colonies like wildfire. I remember it now *verbatim:* "The sun never shined on a cause of greater worth. Everything that is right or reasonable pleads for separation. The blood of the slain, the weeping voice of nature cries, 'TIS TIME TO PART.'"

MODERATOR: Those are powerful words—

ADAMS: —especially for someone who made his living as a corset-maker.

MODERATOR: Well, it was a people's revolution. *(John Dickinson resumes his place at the table. Jefferson stands and helps him into his chair.)* Mr. Dickinson, welcome back.

FRANKLIN: Yes, John, welcome back.

MODERATOR: We were discussing Mr. Paine's pamphlet, *Common Sense,* and how it turned public opinion in favor of independence.

DICKINSON: Yes, I read it.

ADAMS *(to Dickinson, in a conciliatory tone):* If I may say, sir, *Common Sense* was the culmination of our propaganda war against the British, which started nine years before with your *Letters from a Pennsylvania Farmer.* For that we're indebted to you.

DICKINSON: Well, I thank you for that.

MODERATOR: Gentlemen, if we may go back to discussing the *Declaration of Independence—*

ADAMS: Well, Richard Henry Lee of Virginia introduced his resolution for independence on—what day did you say, Ben?

FRANKLIN: The seventh of June.

ADAMS: I remember now. It was late on a Friday afternoon, and the debate was postponed to Saturday.

FRANKLIN: That's right, Saturday morning at 10 o'clock. On the left side of the room were the radicals—you and your cousin Sam and Richard Henry Lee. On the right side were the conservatives—Mr. Dickinson and the others from the middle colonies and Mr. Rutledge of South Carolina. The debate dragged on through the whole weekend.

DICKINSON: I argued that the colonies weren't ripe for the break, that it was better to wait than to force the issue and risk succession.

ADAMS: I argued that independence was already a fact, that a declaration would merely acknowledge it.

FRANKLIN: The issue narrowed to one of timing. Finally, on Monday, the two sides reached a compromise: postpone the vote for three weeks. That gave the middle colonies time to write their assemblies for instructions.

JEFFERSON: That's when I went to work on the *Declaration*. For the next two weeks I buried myself in my rented quarters at Seventh and Market Streets and wrote out the first draft. *(Reaches into his vest.)* Here I have it.

MODERATOR: I wonder, sir, if we could go back to the moment when you read the first draft to Mr. Adams and Dr. Franklin. What date would that have been?

JEFFERSON: Late June of '76.

MODERATOR: would you mind, sir? (*The scene plays out in real time while Jefferson reads from stage left.)*

JEFFERSON: "When in the course of human events it becomes necessary for one people to dissolve the political bands which have connected them with another, and to assume among the powers of the earth the separate and equal station to which the laws of nature and nature's god entitle them, a decent respect to the opinions of mankind requires that they should declare the causes which impel them to the separation."

FRANKLIN: Whoa! I challenge you to diagram that sentence!

JEFFERSON: Do you want me to continue?

FRANKLIN: I'm sorry. Please do.

JEFFERSON: "We hold these truths to be sacred and undeniable: that all men are created equal, that they are endowed by their Creator with certain inalienable rights, that among these are life, liberty, and the pursuit of happiness."

FRANKLIN *(shaking his head)*: Strike "sacred and undeniable"—too dogmatic. Besides it's obvious.

ADAMS *(to Franklin):* Is that the word you want—*obvious?* "We hold these truths to be *obvious*?"

FRANKLIN: Are you familiar with Euclid's *Elements*?

ADAMS: I read them in school. But what in earth does that have to do—

FRANKLIN: "Things that are equal to the same thing are equal to each other." Euclid's first axiom. All of mathematics, he said, is based upon axioms—truths that are self-evident. *(To Jefferson)* May I see that? *(Jefferson hands him his draft.)* "All men are created equal." Hmm. Is that also self-evident? "We hold these truths to be self-evident." *(Hands the paper back to Jefferson.)* Yes, let that be our axiom. *(To Adams)* "Self-evident?"

ADAMS *(nods his assent):* "Self-evident."

JEFFERSON: "Self-evident" it is then. *(Reaches for the quill and makes the correction.)*

FRANKLIN: Go back to the sentence about the king abetting the slave trade to the colonies. How did you phrase that?

JEFFERSON *(flips back a few pages and reads):* "The Christian king of Great Britain has waged cruel war against human nature in the persons of a distant people who never offended him, captivating and carrying them into slavery in another hemisphere."

FRANKLIN: Yes, that's it. You blame the slave trade on the king. In fact that endeavor goes back to the 1500s, long before his time, and it's one in which other countries—Spain, Portugal, the Netherlands—are equally complicit. Moreover, you say nothing of slavery itself. If the slave trade is outlawed, wouldn't the slaves already on our shores become—how shall I put it?—a more lucrative commodity?

JEFFERSON: That wasn't my purpose, Dr. Franklin. Slavery is an insult to human nature. Indeed, I tremble that God's justice cannot sleep forever. But the issue before us is independence, not emancipation.

FRANKLIN *(pauses):* I concede the point.

ADAMS: It is good, sir. Your paper is very good. I admire the high tone and flights of oratory. But my concern is not unlike Dr. Franklin's. In your list of charges you call the king a tyrant. The expression is too personal, too scolding, for so grave and solemn a document. *(Sighs)* But we shall see how it fares on the floor.

JEFFERSON: Thank you, gentlemen, for your comments. *(To the moderator)* That, sir, is more or less how it went.

MODERATOR: Thank you for taking us back to that moment. As I listened, I wondered what your purpose was in writing this document.

JEFFERSON: It wasn't to find out new principles or new arguments never before thought of. It was simply to place before mankind the common sense of the subject. I intended it to be an expression of the American mind. After I read it to Mr. Adams and Dr. Franklin, I made a few more corrections and reported it to the committee.

ADAMS: We were in haste, because Mr. Lee's resolution was coming up for a vote.

MODERATOR: When did that happen?

ADAMS: July 2nd. And it passed unanimously. Mr. Dickinson wasn't there to vote against it.

MODERATOR: So that was the day Congress declared independence.

ADAMS: That's right. That was our first Independence Day: July 2nd, 1776.

FRANKLIN *(to the moderator):* Mr. Adams told me about a letter he wrote to his wife, Abigail, after Lee's motion passed.

ADAMS: Did you have to bring that up, Ben?

FRANKLIN *(teasing)*: What did you say in that letter, John?

ADAMS *(hesitates, then responds):* Well, I told Mrs. Adams that the 2nd day of July, 1776, would be the most memorable epoch in the history of America, that it ought to be celebrated with pomp and parade, with shows, games, sports, guns, bells, bonfires, and illuminations from one end of the continent to the other, from this time forward, forevermore. *(Sighs)* July the 2nd.

MODERATOR: Well, sir, you were only two days off.

ADAMS *(to the moderator)*: Mr. Lee's resolution notwithstanding, the fact that you celebrate Independence Day on July 4th, not July 2nd, is testimony to the power of the written word.

MODERATOR: So what happened after Mr. Lee's resolution passed?

ADAMS: We took up debate on Mr. Jefferson's draft. And let me tell you, there is nothing worse than turning a roomful of lawyers loose on a piece of paper. They fell on it like a pack of wolves. For three days they tore away at it, ripping out offensive words and phrases as if they were cancerous tissue. *(Franklin appears to be dozing.)* My colleague here, Dr. Franklin, slept through most of it.

FRANKLIN *(startled)*: Now, now John. I listened to every word you spoke in defense of Mr. Jefferson's paper. It's just that my ears work better when my eyes are closed.

ADAMS: Well, I argued myself hoarse while Mr. Jefferson suffered in silence. Of the eighteen hundred words in his draft Congress struck out no less than a fourth, including the passage we talked about accusing the King of abetting the slave trade. Our colleagues from Georgia and the Carolinas would have nothing of that.

FRANKLIN*:* Tom, do you remember the story I told you about John Thompson?

JEFFERSON: John Thompson?

FRANKLIN: Yes, John Thompson. He ran a hat shop in Philadelphia. I could see how distraught you were while Congress hacked away at your paper. So I told you about a sign Mr. Thompson made for his shop that said, "John Thompson, Hatter, Makes and Sells Hats for Ready Money," and it displayed a hat. He showed the sign to his friends and they all hacked away at it. One of them said, "What do you mean, '*sells* hats?' Nobody expects you to *give* them away!" Mr. Thompson's sign ended up with just his name and the hat.

JEFFERSON: Yes, I do remember now. I confess the point was lost on me at the time.

ADAMS: Well, the slashing went on for three days. By the evening of the 4th—it was a Thursday and, my lord, was it hot. We had closed the windows to keep the deliberations private. Finally, John Hancock ordered a final reading of Jefferson's paper and called for the vote. *(To Franklin)* Do you remember how it went?

FRANKLIN: Twelve colonies voted yea. New York abstained because they hadn't yet received instructions from their assembly.

ADAMS: Again, Mr. Dickinson stayed home.

MODERATOR: So when did New York vote?

FRANKLIN: July 15. That's when it became unanimous.

MODERATOR: So I take it the *Declaration* wasn't signed on the 4th of July.

FRANKLIN: That's right. We passed it on the 4th, but we didn't sign it till later. We held the first public reading on July 8th, in the yard outside the Pennsylvania State House. My, what a scene that was. Thousands of citizens embraced and cheered.

MODERATOR: Did anybody know that Mr. Jefferson had written it?

FRANKLIN: Nobody outside the Congress. I think he preferred it that way because he was upset by what Congress had done to it.

MODERATOR: Is that true, Mr. Jefferson?

JEFFERSON: Yes. They mangled it.

ADAMS *(to Jefferson):* Pride goeth before the fall, Tom, including pride of authorship. But I did my best to defend your work.

JEFFERSON: You did, sir, and I'm grateful to you for that. *(To the moderator)* But I was distraught for another reason.

MODERATOR: What was that?

JEFFERSON: My wife. As I mentioned, our infant daughter had recently died and my wife was under great distress when I left home. The only thing keeping me in Philadelphia was a sense of duty. I couldn't wait for my replacement to arrive so I could return home.

MODERATOR *(to Dickinson):* And you, sir, had to have some anxiety of your own. It is true that you refused to sign the *Declaration of Independence?*

DICKINSON: Yes, that's true. But I want Mr. Adams to know that since I could not in good conscience remain a delegate to Congress, I resigned from that distinguished body and became a brigadier general in the Pennsylvania militia. (*Turns to Adams*) Sir, I want you to know that I, too, joined the fight for independence.

ADAMS: So, my friend, you redeemed yourself!

MODERATOR: On that note, gentlemen, I think we should wrap this up.

FRANKLIN: Ah, but Mr. Jefferson is about to favor us with a tune.

MODERATOR *(to Jefferson):* Sir, what are you going to play for us?

JEFFERSON: Something short. I sent to London for this before the boycott, a composition by George Friedrich Handel. It's titled, "*La rejouisssance.*" *(Jefferson plays the first few measures and bows while the others thump the table.)*

MODERATOR *(facing the audience)*: Well, my friends, that's what happened in 1776, the year of the founding of the new United States of America. Please join me in thanking our guests—Dr. Benjamin Franklin, Mr. Thomas Jefferson, Mr. John Adams, and Mr. John Dickinson. Thank you for joining us. Have a happy Fourth of July. Or is it the Second of July? Whatever. Have a good night and God bless.

EPISODE 2

Making a Government

The Untold Story of the U.S. Constitution

STAGING NOTE

Like Episode 1, Episode 2 takes place in the present, but the Founders appear as they would have sometime after the 1787 Constitutional Convention and should be aged accordingly: Alexander Hamilton about 35, James Madison and Gouverneur Morris about 40, George Washington about 60, and Benjamin Franklin about 80. The set is the same as in Episode 1.

CAST OF CHARACTERS

JAMES MADISON (1751-1836). Delegate from Virginia. Today we remember him as the Father of the Constitution more than as the fourth president of the United States. Slight-of-build, high-strung and persnickety, he had an obsession to detail that proved to be a good thing: His handwritten journal is the most complete record we have of the Constitutional Convention. Of all the delegates he was the most politically astute. His Virginia Plan became largely the model for the new Constitution.

ALEXANDER HAMILTON (1755?-1804). Delegate from New York. John Adams called him "the bastard brat of a Scottish peddler." Born out of wedlock, he left his native West Indies as a teenager to seek his fortune in North America. Ambitious and highly intelligent, he reveled in the Revolution and rose through the military ranks to become General Washington's aide-de-camp. In the Convention his prickly disposition and outspoken fondness for British monarchy alienated many of his fellow delegates.

BENJAMIN FRANKLIN (1706-1790). Delegate from Pennsylvania. Supported by a cane, his long hair trailing over his shoulder, he personified philosophic tranquility. His wisdom and wit often eased tensions among the delegates. Notes historian Richard Beeman: "Franklin's contributions to the debates...were often quirky, but his final speech, urging the delegates to put the need for a harmonious union above their own interests... marked a decisive moment in the process of making the Constitution."

GOUVERNEUR MORRIS (1752-1816). Delegate from Pennsylvania. Born into a family of wealth and privilege, Morris had the demeanor of an aristocrat and the life style of a rogue. He was fond of spirits and pleasures of the flesh; he walked with a wooden leg, the consequence of a romantic tryst. At the Constitutional Convention he spoke more often—and more bombastically—than any other delegate. Yet he was a gifted writer. Few people today know that it was he who wrote the final draft of the Constitution.

GEORGE WASHINGTON (1732-1799). President of the Convention (cameo appearance). Having reluctantly agreed to attend the Convention and skeptical of its outcome, Washington did not miss a single day of the proceedings. Although he barely uttered a word during the debates, his charismatic presence and evenhandedness in presiding over the deliberations cemented his reputation as America's "indispensable man."

EPISODE 2

Making A Government

MODERATOR: Welcome to Episode 2 of *Inventing America*. In the first episode, "Making a Nation," we talked about how the thirteen American colonies declared their independence from Great Britain. That historic event took place at the Pennsylvania State House in Philadelphia—what we now call Independence Hall—in July of 1776. Tonight, we return to the State House, but it's eleven years later—the summer of 1787.

The colonies did indeed make good on their Declaration of Independence. The Continental Army under General George Washington drove out the British, and the thirteen colonies formed a new nation under the Articles of Confederation. But things did not work out quite the way they had hoped. What happened? Well, tonight we will find out. We will also find out what our Founders did about it—and how it changed the world.

Each of our guests tonight took part in the momentous debates between May and September, 1787, a mere four months that determined the fate of the new United States of America. Their mission was to create a working government. Our first guest was so eager to get on with this business that he showed up eleven days early. And while he waited for everyone else, he drew up a plan. The question was would it work? Or would it be another failed attempt at self-government? We begin our conversation with the great little man from Virginia. We also know him as the Father of our Constitution and the fourth President of the United

States. Please welcome Mr. James Madison. *(Madison enters with a satchel of books, looking disoriented.)* Please have a seat, Mr. President.

MADISON: May I lie down?

MODERATOR: Lie down? I don't think we have a sofa.

MADISON: Well, I talk better when I'm lying, but since you don't have a sofa I guess I'll have to sit. *(He drops the satchel beside his chair and sits down.)*

MODERATOR: So you talk better when you're lying. I thought you always told the truth.

MADISON: I did. So did George Washington. He never told a lie. You know the story about his father's cherry tree.

MODERATOR: Of course. Every schoolchild does.

MADISON: Well, the story was a lie. It never happened. But the moral was true. You could not—would not, God forbid—tell a lie in 18th Century Virginia.

MODERATOR: Why not?

MADISON: Because under English law you'd get your ears nailed to a pillory followed by twenty lashes on the back.

MODERATOR: That sounds like cruel and unusual punishment.

MADISON: Look it up—Statutes of Virginia, 1723, Volume 127. Mr. Jefferson, my mentor, showed it to me. Have you seen his library at Monticello? It's quite magnificent.

MODERATOR: So Thomas Jefferson was your mentor.

MADISON: Indeed he was. It was Mr. Jefferson who got me interested in changing archaic laws like that one that stemmed from monarchial rule. I was but twenty-five years old when I came under his influence. It happened while I helped him draft a new constitution for the State of Virginia in 1776, the year we declared independence. I have to admit I was quite impressionable.

MODERATOR: At twenty-five shouldn't you have been fighting in Washington's army?

MADISON: Sir, it's no fluke they called me Little Jemmy Madison from Virginia. I was frail, slight of build, of nervous temperament, prone to anxiety attacks, *and* allergic to dust.

MODERATOR: So you were 4-F.

MADISON: Beg pardon?

MODERATOR: 4-F. It's a ranking for military fitness.

MADISON: I see. In any case I wasn't fit for military service, so I went into politics. Thanks to Mr. Jefferson I got elected to the Federal Convention in Philadelphia since he couldn't come.

MODERATOR: Why not?

MADISON: Because he was in Paris serving as envoy to France. But we agreed to stay in touch. He wanted to keep a hand in this business, even from across the Atlantic.

MODERATOR: You said punishments like pillorying and whipping stemmed from monarchial rule. Can you explain?

MADISON: Those things were mild compared to other punishments. For example, the punishment for slander was to have a spike driven through your tongue. For burglary, it was to have your body broken on a wheel. Abolishing cruel and unusual punishments was just one of the things we accomplished in a new Declaration of Rights for Virginia. It was part of our new state constitution. Another was assuring freedom of religion and the press; another, trial by jury. I helped George Mason write the Virginia Declaration of Rights, just as I'd helped Mr. Jefferson write our new state constitution. It was partly the model for our work in Philadelphia.

MODERATOR: The so-called Virginia Plan.

MADISON: Call it what you will. I got our governor, Edmund Randolph, to introduce it, so you could also call it the Randolph Plan. Somebody even called it Little Jemmy's Big Bright Idea. But it stirred up objections from the start.

MODERATOR: How come?

MADISON: Because making a new federal constitution wasn't our mandate. Our mandate was to revise the Articles of Confederation, which the Continental Congress had adopted after declaring independence.

MODERATOR: What was wrong with them?

MADISON: The Articles served us well enough in wartime when we were united against a common enemy. But when the cannon smoke cleared they proved woefully inadequate. They did little more than unite the states in name. Each state coined its own money, levied its own taxes, conducted its own foreign policy. In Virginia we had our own Treaty of Amity with France. But we had an even bigger problem.

MODERATOR: You did?

MADISON: Indeed. The Virginia Plan was considered radical because it was based on republican principles. The term itself—"republican" with a small "r"—was pejorative. It was a term one used to attack the credibility of one's political opponent.

MODERATOR: That's hard to grasp when we have so many republics today.

MADISON: Ah, but in the 18th century monarchy was the rule. It had been for centuries. Talk about cruel and unusual punishment. Monarchies ruled by blood in more ways than one. That was how they stayed in power.

MODERATOR: I see.

MADISON: Do you read the Bible?

MODERATOR *(shrugs)*: Well, I—

MADISON: Look, even the Bible endorsed monarchy. Look at I Samuel, Chapter 8. The ancient Israelites demanded a king like every other nation. Monarchy had history on its side. Rome had a republic for a while, but it didn't last. England tried it in the 17th century, but it ended with a dictator. So when we came to Philadelphia we knew the odds were against us. We were about to do something that would change the world. Yet Mr. Hamilton, my colleague from New York whose idea it was to get people together and try to figure out what to do about this—he had trouble getting people just to show up.

MODERATOR: Well, let's ask him about that. *(Faces the audience.)*

Indeed, our next guest was the one most responsible for organizing the Constitutional Convention. Born in the West Indies, he came to North America as a young man, received his education at King's College in New York—what is now Columbia University—and distinguished himself in the Continental Army as an aide-de-camp to General Washington. Later he founded our nation's financial system as our first Secretary of the Treasury. Would you welcome, please, from the State of New York, Mr. Alexander Hamilton. *(Hamilton enters and sits down.)* It's an honor, sir—if not a miracle—to have you on the program.

HAMILTON *(eyes him suspiciously)*: I'm not sure what you mean by that, but thank you.

MODERATOR: If I'm not mistaken, you weren't the only delegate to the Convention who wasn't American-born.

HAMILTON: That depends on how you define American. Seven of the delegates were British-born. They were upper crust in the old British tradition. I wasn't. Now, was I American-born? You tell me. I was born on the island of Nevis in the Caribbean. It was so tiny and insignificant that Columbus didn't bother to explore it. But I was looked down upon not because of the *place* of my birth but the *circumstances*.

MODERATOR: Circumstances?

HAMILTON: My birth was the subject of the most humiliating criticism. I didn't know who my father was. Nor did I know the year I was born. Do you know what John Adams called me?

MODERATOR: No, what did he call you?

HAMILTON: "The bastard brat of a Scottish peddler." That's what he called me.

MODERATOR: Most people say things they want to take back.

HAMILTON: Well, he never did. *(Sighs)* It's just as well he went to England.

MODERATOR: Why did he go there?

HAMILTON: Congress appointed him minister to the Court of Saint James's—God help us. At least he confined his mischief to London.

MODERATOR: Chances are America wouldn't be independent today without Mr. Adams.

HAMILTON: People said the same of Jefferson in my day. It's just as well he stayed in France. I never had much use for him either.

MADISON *(to Hamilton):* Careful what you say about Mr. Jefferson.

HAMILTON: I beg your pardon, sir. I forget that you were one of his...acolytes. *(Madison stiffens.)*

MODERATOR: Mr. Hamilton, you were describing the circumstances of your birth.

HAMILTON: Yes. The man I assumed was my father—the Scottish peddler as Adams called him—deserted my mother when I was a lad. They were never legally married. After that my mother moved to the island of Saint Croix with my older brother and me and supported us by keeping a shop. Then she contracted a fever and died.

MODERATOR: How old were you?

HAMILTON: Eleven, twelve perhaps. I passed myself off as thirteen so I could find employment. My brother and I were adopted by a cousin who later committed suicide. After that we were separated and never saw each other again.

MODERATOR: How sad.

HAMILTON: Next I was adopted by a merchant who I came to suspect was my real father. His name was Thomas Stevens.

MODERATOR: Why did you think *he* was your father?

HAMILTON: Because he had a son, Edward, who many said looked very much like me. Edward and I were the best of friends if not half brothers. My real name could be Alexander Stevens, not Alexander Hamilton.

MODERATOR: I take it he never let on.

HAMILTON: He didn't, but thanks to his connections I found employment as a clerk at an import-export firm on the island. When the owner left on vacation he put me in charge. That was my introduction to business and finance; it opened my eyes to the world. When I was sixteen, perhaps seventeen or eighteen—I was never certain of my age—I sailed to Boston and never looked back.

MODERATOR: So you came to North America by yourself, as a teenager—

HAMILTON: —and an orphan. General Washington was the closest thing I had to a father. There was no one to whom I was more indebted for my good fortune.

MODERATOR: So you came here as an orphan. How did you meet General Washington?

HAMILTON: After the first shot was fired at Lexington I joined a volunteer militia in New York. Most of us were King's College students. I raised an artillery company, fought in several battles, and rose through the ranks to become General Washington's aide-de-camp. Before long he had me drafting letters to the Congress, to his generals and governors of the states. He even had me issue orders in his name.

MODERATOR: He must have placed great trust in you.

HAMILTON: He did, and I reciprocated with diligence and loyalty. He was, as I said, like a father to me.

MODERATOR: How long did you serve as his aide-de-camp?

HAMILTON: Four years, right up to Cornwallis's surrender at Yorktown. I knew how frustrated the general was with the scant support he received from Congress, yet we won the war. It wasn't until Yorktown that I learned firsthand how powerless Congress was.

MODERATOR: How did you find out?

HAMILTON: When I sent a messenger to deliver the news of our victory to Congress, he told me on his return that Congress didn't have enough money to pay his expenses. So each member contributed a dollar from his own pocket.

MODERATOR: That's a pretty loose way to do business.

HAMILTON: Under the Articles of Confederation, Congress had neither purse nor sword to govern the thirteen states. It had no taxing authority. It relied solely on voluntary contributions.

MADISON *(to the moderator):* Sir, may I interject something?

MODERATOR: Of course.

MADISON: It was not just Congress's inability to tax that was the rub. It was that states acted out of self-interest to the detriment of their neighbors. New Jersey, for example, situated between Philadelphia and New York, was like a cask tapped at both ends. North Carolina, situated between Virginia and South Carolina, was like a *(pauses, searching for the right words)* patient bleeding at both arms.

HAMILTON: So Madison, are you saying that when your state, Virginia, seized vessels for non-payment of duties that this action was aimed not at England or Spain but at New York?

MADISON *(agitated)*: What I am saying sir is that most political evils stem from commercial ones. I admit that my state was no less guilty than yours. Wasn't that what brought us here?

MODERATOR *(in a calming tone)*: Well, gentlemen, it certainly was *one* of the reasons.

HAMILTON *(softens, looking at the moderator but gesturing toward Madison)*: We did try to correct the situation at Annapolis the year before, but it didn't work out. Do you know how many delegates showed up?

MODERATOR: No.

HAMILTON: Twelve—twelve delegates from five states. That included present company. We couldn't even raise a quorum. The country was in a malaise. So we decided to call another convention. I doubt we could have pulled it off without Shays' Rebellion.

MODERATOR: Shays' Rebellion?

HAMILTON: Yes, it started in Massachusetts about the same time we met at Annapolis. It was a protest led by a former army captain named Daniel Shays against the seizure of farms for debts incurred during the war. Shays and his men marched with staves and pitchforks on county courthouses and frightened people out of their wits. Congress asked the states for money and troops to quell the rebellion, but the request was ignored.

MODERATOR: As you said, Congress had neither purse nor sword.

HAMILTON: Anarchy was in the air. *(He removes a letter from his vest.)* I quote from a letter General Washington sent from Mount Vernon after he got the news from Massachusetts. *(He unfolds the letter and reads.)* "The United States exhibit melancholy proof of what our transatlantic foe"—he's referring to England, our mother country "what our transatlantic foe predicted: that mankind is unfit to govern itself."

MODERATOR: That must have been discouraging.

HAMILTON: Ah, but Shays' Rebellion was a blessing in disguise; it spurred us to action. So we set another date, May 14, 1787, to meet in Philadelphia.

MODERATOR: Did all thirteen states show up this time?

HAMILTON: Twelve of the thirteen did. Rhode Island—or as I prefer to call her, *Rogue Island*—stayed home.

MADISON *(removes a notebook from his satchel)*: According to my journal, twelve states appointed seventy-four delegates. Of that number fifty-five showed up.

MODERATOR: Let's see, that's means nineteen *didn't* show up. That's more than a fourth.

HAMILTON: And most of those who did were late, including Dr. Franklin. We had arranged for him to nominate General Washington as president of the convention. When he didn't show up we had to get Robert Morris to do it.

MADISON *(consulting his notebook)*: Seven states—just enough for a quorum—were seated on May 25th. That's when the proceedings began.

MODERATOR *(to Hamilton)*: I'm curious why the religiously early-to-bed, early-to-rise Dr. Franklin was late.

HAMILTON: Well, you'll have to ask *him*.

MODERATOR: He's waiting back stage so I think I will. *(Faces the audience.)* Ladies and gentlemen, it's an honor to have on our program one of the world's preeminent philosopher-statesmen, scientists, and inventors. After serving as our country's Minister to France, he came home and found himself back in his old seat at the Pennsylvania State House. But this time it wasn't to birth a nation; it was to help figure out how to run it. Please welcome the first citizen of Philadelphia, Dr. Benjamin Franklin.

FRANKLIN *(enters with a cane, spots a young lady in the front row)*: Hello my dear! Oh, to be seventy again!

MODERATOR: Welcome back, sir. I was afraid you might not make it this time.

FRANKLIN: It seems I'm late for everything as I get older. *(Sits down with a groan.)* Just call me the late Doctor Franklin.

MADISON: Better late than never, Doctor Franklin.

FRANKLIN: My dear Madison, I shan't be *late* as long as I can sit. Besides, it's better to die...*lying*.

MODERATOR: Well, sir, I'm just glad you're here.

FRANKLIN: I want to show you something. *(Hands the moderator a sketch.)* A sedan chair—a gift from Marie-Antoinette. It's how I maneuvered the cobbled streets of Versailles. It was easier on my gout than a carriage.

MODERATOR: I'm impressed. *(Hands the sketch back to Franklin.)*

FRANKLIN: Well, it did make it less painful to get around. *(Turns to Hamilton.)* Sir, you mentioned Annapolis where twelve delegates showed up. That wasn't the first time we tried to establish a federal union. We tried it in Albany at the beginning of the French and Indian War, in 1754. Our purpose was to establish a common defense against the French. That was before Her Majesty took a shine to me.

MADISON: Long before, I would say. In 1754 Marie-Antoinette was an infant.

FRANKLIN *(smiles wryly)*: I stand corrected. Just the same, at Albany I proposed a Plan of Union with a president appointed by the Crown.

MODERATOR: What happened?

FRANKLIN: The plan was rejected. The colonies weren't ready to give up their sovereignty. But that wasn't the worst of it.

MODERATOR: Oh?

FRANKLIN: The trip home nearly killed me. The boat I was in going down the Hudson sprang a leak and sank. Luckily, I made it to shore.

MODERATOR: So the Albany Plan went down with your boat.

FRANKLIN: As I said, travel for me was difficult, especially in my later years. *(Sighs)* You think I would have learned my lesson.

MODERATOR: But at the Constitutional Convention you were three blocks from home, Dr. Franklin.

FRANKLIN: That's true. I'd seen more of the world than most, but at my age it was an ordeal just to cross the street.

MODERATOR: So why were you late?

FRANKLIN: The gout, my friend, and the rain. Like mercury and water, they don't mix. So I stayed in bed. I had the same affliction during the Second Continental Congress. Otherwise, mind you, it might well have been yours truly, not Mr. Jefferson, who wrote the Declaration of Independence.

MODERATOR: Speaking of Mr. Jefferson, didn't he replace you as Minister to France?

MADISON: "Succeeded" was the word he used when he wrote *me* about it. He said Dr. Franklin could not be "replaced."

FRANKLIN (*flattered*): Well, wasn't that generous of him! Speaking of generosity, I must say Mr. Jefferson was as generous with the French ladies as I was.

MADISON: With due respect, sir, he was a bit younger than you... and a widower.

FRANKLIN *(to the moderator)*: Before I returned from France I noticed a young lady to whom he was paying close attention. She wasn't a Frenchwoman but a mulatto who appeared to have recently come of age—a maid servant to his daughter, no less. Oh, what was her name? He called her...Sally.

MODERATOR: Yes, we know about Sally Hemings.

FRANKLIN: Is that so? Well, it's hard to keep these things quiet, you know. The whole world knew about my illegitimate son, William, who become the royal governor of New Jersey and then went to England as a loyalist. His deserting me in my old age grieved me to my dying day. Then there was Gouverneur Morris, my fellow delegate from Pennsylvania, the one with the wooden leg.

MODERATOR: He happens to be our next guest.

FRANKLIN: Well then, let *him* tell you about his wooden leg.

MODERATOR: I think I will. *(Faces the audience.)* Our next guest is one of our lesser known founding fathers but deserves a place in our history because of the crucial role he played at the Constitutional Convention. He not only gave more speeches than anybody else—

MADISON *(consulting his journal)*: —one hundred and seventy-three—

MODERATOR: —thank you—one hundred and seventy-three speeches—but he proved his skill with the written word as well. He is the unsung hero of the U.S. Constitution as well as one of the more colorful characters behind it. Would you welcome, please, from the State of Pennsylvania, Mr. Gouverneur Morris. *(Morris enters with a scroll rolled up in his hand.)*

MODERATOR: Thank you for joining us.

MORRIS: My pleasure. It's nice to be recognized finally. *(Lays the scroll on the table and sits down.)*

MODERATOR: Dr. Franklin mentioned your wooden leg. If you'll pardon my impertinence, sir, may I ask how you, uh, came to acquire it? *(Morris appears slightly taken back)*

FRANKLIN *(teasing)*: Tell him, Gouv. It could have happened to any of us, except Madison perhaps. He was too strait laced to get into any such fix as you did.

MORRIS: Well, I, uh, got run over by a carriage. *(Pauses.)*

FRANKLIN: Go on. Tell him the rest of the story.

MORRIS: I was jumping out of a window.

FRANKLIN: And why, pray tell, were you doing that? *(He glances at Hamilton, who breaks into a grin.)*

MORRIS: Are you asking me to testify against myself?

FRANKLIN: This isn't a court of law, Gouv. Nor am I a lawyer. Perhaps Mr. Hamilton should be asking you these questions.

MORRIS *(draws in his breath):* All right, I jumped out the window when the husband of the lady I was, uh, *visiting*...entered the room. I landed out on the street. *(Franklin and Hamilton break into laughter. Madison glares at them.)*

HAMILTON: Obviously, Madison doesn't see the humor in this.

MADISON: I don't!

FRANKLIN *(to Madison)*: Well, my bachelor friend, as I told you back in 1787, I suspected there would be *(rolls his eyes)* a *dolly* in your future one day, and I expressed the hope that she would be as worthy of you as you would be of her.

MADISON: I do remember, Dr. Franklin. Thank you.

MODERATOR: Gentlemen, you just proved something important. Too often we think of you, our founding fathers, as marbled saints when in fact you were normal human beings with normal human frailties like the rest of us. Somehow I find that...comforting.

MADISON: Ah, but when I told Mr. Jefferson about our Convention, he called us "an assembly of demigods." *(The other three break into laughter.)*

FRANKLIN: I don't know whether the gentleman spoke in reverence or in jest, but human nature is what it is—

MODERATOR: —which brings us back to the constitution. People constantly complain about government, how it controls their lives. Why do we need it?

MADISON: If men were angels, no government would be necessary.

MODERATOR: Can you elaborate?

MADISON: The reason we need government is that we're men, not angels. The great difficulty in framing a government administered by men is this: First you must enable the government to control the governed, and then you must oblige it to control itself.

MODERATOR: How did you accomplish that?

MADISON: We didn't. Our constitution is—always will be—a work in progress.

MODERATOR: So tell me how you began.

MADISON: Well, as I said, we started with the Virginia Plan. It called for two legislative chambers, an upper house and a lower house—similar to the British Parliament.

MODERATOR: I guess old traditions die hard.

MADISON: Independence from Britain didn't rule out our adopting worthy elements of her government for our own. That included a bicameral legislature, the lower house to be elected by the people, the upper house to be elected by the lower house. The Virginia Plan also called for a separate executive and judiciary. Mr. Jefferson and I proposed these ideas for the Virginia Constitution and they were accepted. So I asked myself, might the same ideas with a few modifications be proposed for a *federal* constitution as well?

MODERATOR: Was the Virginia Constitution your only model for the federal government?

MADISON: Good heavens, no. I wrote Mr. Jefferson in Paris and asked him if he would send me books about ancient and modern confederacies that might throw light on the subject. Before I knew it, books started arriving by the box load—histories and biographies, books on political theory and the laws of nations. He sent me books by Burlamaqui and Montesquieu and d'Albon and Rousseau. Some were years out of print. *(Reaches into his satchel)* Here's one I haven't read yet, Voltaire's *Treatise on Tolerance*, 1763. *(He places the book on the table.)*

FRANKLIN *(brightens)*: May I see it? I had the pleasure of making Voltaire's acquaintance when I was Minister to France. *(Franklin picks up the book, opens it, and blows off the dust. This launches Madison into a coughing fit.)*

FRANKLIN: Oh dear, I forgot you're allergic to dust.

MODERATOR *(to Madison)*: May I get you a glass of water?

MORRIS *(reaches into his coat for a flask and shot glass):* Here, try this. *(Morris pours the ingredients into the shot glass and passes it down to Madison who shakes his head and continues coughing)*

MORRIS: Drink up. It helped *me* when I lost my leg.

MADISON *(still coughing)*: What is it?

MORRIS: West Indian rum. What island it comes from I don't know. All I know is that it works. *(Madison hesitates before taking a sip, and then gulps down the rest. He returns the shot glass to the table with a clunk.)*

MORRIS: I bet Hamilton could tell you where it comes from.

HAMILTON *(picks up the shot glass and sniffs it):* Saint Croix... Cruzan. I used to export this stuff.

MORRIS: Let's have Dr. Franklin try it. *(Pours another glass and passes it to Franklin.)*

FRANKLIN *(sips the rum and swirls it his mouth)*: Sorry, not to my taste. *(He offers it to the moderator.)* Would you like some?

MODERATOR: No, thank you. I'm working.

FRANKLIN: Do you think we're *not* working?

MODERATOR: Well, weren't you paid for the work you did?

FRANKLIN: No, we served the public without pay. As citizens we were fulfilling our obligation to public service. *(To Morris with a twinkle)* It also meant nobody could fire us. *(Morris removes another flask from his coat and takes a drink.)*

MODERATOR: Gentlemen, if we may return to the subject at hand.

FRANKLIN: Yes, of course. Because we lacked a quorum I invited the gentlemen at this table along with General Washington and a few others to come to my home on Market Street. There under a mulberry tree in my courtyard we discussed Mr. Madison's plan over a cask of *fine*

French wine. (Franklin casts a sideways glance to Morris.) We assented to Mr. Madison's plan in principle and discussed how we might present it at the Convention.

HAMILTON: That assumed we wouldn't be left high and dry again.

MADISON: Finally, on May 25th, we had enough delegates for a quorum. The first order of business was to elect General Washington to preside; the second was to vote on a motion from Mr. Hamilton to conduct our business in secret. I didn't agree with it, nor did Mr. Jefferson when I informed him of the outcome.

HAMILTON *(to Madison)*: Look, had the deliberations been open, the clamors of faction would have prevented any satisfactory result. Had they been disclosed afterwards, much fuel would have been fed to inflammatory declamation. Even the General insisted that nothing be printed or communicated to the outside. Otherwise, how could we have freely debated?

MODERATOR: So the deliberations took place behind closed doors. *(To Madison)* When did you present the Virginia Plan?

MADISON: That came next. We had broken the plan down into fifteen Resolves. Then Governor Randolph offered them as *suggestions* from the Virginia delegation.

MODERATOR: That sounds like a good start.

MADISON: Not a voice rose in protest. For a moment I thought all fifteen Resolves would pass without debate and we'd go home with a new government. Not so. After the weight of what had been presented settled in, all hell broke loose.

MODERATOR: What happened?

MADISON: Charles Pinckney of South Carolina accused us of violating our mandate from Congress, which was merely to revise the Articles of Confederation.

MODERATOR: You alluded to that earlier.

MADISON: Then others joined the attack. Did we intend to abolish the state governments in favor of a *national* government?

HAMILTON: Fortunately, my friend Mr. Morris came to the rescue on that one.

MORRIS: I argued that what was being proposed was a *federal* government, not a *national* one; that a *federal* government was nothing more than a compact that rested on the good faith of the consenting parties. A *national* government, on the other hand, would be a complete and compulsive operation. *(He grins cynically and swipes another drink)*

FRANKLIN: You always had a way with words, Gouv.

MORRIS *(warming to the occasion)*: I argued that when the powers of the *national* government clashed with the states, only then must the states yield. Better to take a *supreme* government now than a despot twenty years hence.

MODERATOR: *National...federal...supreme.* You throw all these terms around to describe a central government. Don't they mean the same thing? I'm confused.

FRANKLIN: Don't think *we* weren't! When we finally arrived at a distinction, we found ourselves split into two groups: the *Federalists* and the *Nationalists.* The smaller states—Connecticut, Delaware, Maryland and New Jersey—wanted to continue the loose federation of states with only minor changes. The larger states—Massachusetts, North Carolina, Pennsylvania and Virginia—wanted a strong national government. The rest stood in between.

MADISON: The delegates agreed in principle to the two houses of Congress. But the agreement broke down when we took up debate on how the two houses should be represented. The smaller states wanted equal representation from all the states—one state, one vote. The larger states wanted proportional representation based on population. They insisted on the same rule in the upper house, which we called the Senate.

MODERATOR *(in jest):* Not the House of Lords?

MADISON *(mildly indignant)*: Our emulating the British stopped short of governance by inheritance.

MODERATOR: So how did you come up with the term *Senate*?

MADISON: We borrowed it from the Romans.

MORRIS *(to the moderator):* You know what it means, don't you? It comes from the Latin word *senex*—"old man"—same as the word *senile. (Swipes another drink)*

MADISON: Well, our purpose wasn't to stack the Senate with senile old men. Rather it was to provide a forum for wise *(casts a reproving glance to Morris)* and *sober* consideration of legislation passed by the lower house—like a council of elders. This idea didn't just go back to the Romans. It went back to earliest civilization.

MODERATOR: You said the upper house was to be chosen by the lower house, not by the people. You're not talking about pure democracy here.

MADISON: Mr. Morris distinguishes between a *federal* government and a *national* government. We need to distinguish also between a *democracy* and a *republic.*

MODERATOR: You mean they're not the same thing either?

MADISON: Not exactly. A democracy gives power *directly* to the people. A republic gives power to those *chosen* by the people. That's where age and wisdom come in.

HAMILTON *(to Madison)*: A democracy doesn't permit vigorous execution. It is therefore bad.

FRANKLIN: But is there any better form? *(All heads turn to Hamilton, who doesn't answer.)*

MODERATOR: So, gentlemen, how did you solve the representation issue?

FRANKLIN: We didn't. William Patterson of New Jersey offered an alternative to Mr. Madison's plan. It called for one house with one vote per state, which I favored, and an executive without veto power, which I opposed.

MADISON: The debate on Mr. Patterson's plan did no more than impede our progress. After three days we voted it down, which put us back to square one. We took up the Virginia Plan again with its two houses of Congress. Oliver Ellsworth of Connecticut, on behalf of the smaller states, moved once more to drop the notion of a Senate based on popular representation. He insisted that each state in the upper house, regardless of size, should have one vote. On that point he wouldn't yield. We were at an impasse.

MORRIS *(inebriated)*: Alas, the fate of America suspended by a hair!

MADISON: Then Dr. Franklin did something that confounded us all. He implored us to seek divine intervention.

FRANKLIN: Gentlemen, if I may. When you assemble a number of men to gain the advantage of their joint wisdom, you inevitably assemble with them all their prejudices, their passions, their errors of opinion, and their selfish views. Moreover, the longer I live the more convinced I am that God governs in the affairs of men. If a sparrow can't fall to the ground without his notice, is it probable that a nation can rise without his aid? So yes, gentlemen, I did implore the House to look to heaven for assistance.

HAMILTON *(to Franklin)*: The last thing we needed was foreign aid. To me it was madness to trust the future to miracles.

MODERATOR *(to Franklin)*: Amidst all this rancor how did you manage to hold the House together?

FRANKLIN: General Washington. His silence spoke louder than most men's words. I never knew a crowned head in Europe whose bearing or demeanor equaled his. He was every inch a general. Did you ever notice, gentlemen, how, through the slightest gesture or gaze of the eye, he would signal to people in his presence to keep a respectful distance?

MORRIS: Nonsense! His demeanor never intimidated me in the least.

HAMILTON *(to Morris)*: Well, then, I propose a wager with you, my friend: dinner for our respective delegates. Should you greet the general with a slap on the back the next time you see him, I pay. Should you not, you pay. Agreed? (*Hamilton stands to shake Morris's hand.)*

MORRIS *(stands, a bit unsteady, reaches in front of Franklin's face and shakes Hamilton's hand):* Agreed. The next time I see the general I shall greet him so.

HAMILTON: Dr. Franklin, you're witness to this wager, right?

FRANKLIN: Do I have a choice?

MODERATOR *(to Madison)*: So what happened after Dr. Franklin asked for divine intervention?

MADISON: The general—the president, rather—tabled Mr. Ellsworth's motion on behalf of the smaller states. That gave everybody a few days to cool off. Then we took up debate on the executive branch: how many executives should be chosen, how they should be chosen, how long they should serve, how much should they be paid. Some wanted a three-man executive council. Others wanted a single executive chosen by Congress.

FRANKLIN: I argued that the executive as well as members of Congress should serve without pay.

MODERATOR: What was your rationale for that?

FRANKLIN: I argued that the common good would be better served by men of public virtue than by swine feeding at the public trough. I had seen enough of that in London.

MORRIS *(to Franklin)*: Didn't you say something about the twelve apostles serving without pay?

FRANKLIN: I did. And indeed *they* did. But later I observed how ecclesiastical benefices from that humble beginning had grown to the whole complex edifice of the papal system. So in the end I did agree to the payment of a modest stipend.

HAMILTON: In my opinion the crucial question before the House was not how much the executive should be paid, but rather how he should be chosen. And what should be the limit of his power? Then I asked to take the floor to make a proposal.

MODERATOR: Take us back to that moment. What date are you talking about?

FRANKLIN: I'm sure Mr. Madison wrote it down.

MADISON *(checking his journal)*: Let's see, Mr. Hamilton came forward with his proposal on June 18, 1787. *(All eyes turn to Hamilton as the following scene plays out in real time.)*

HAMILTON *(rises from his chair and clears his throat)*: My situation is disagreeable, gentlemen, but it would be criminal not to come forward on a question of such magnitude. *(He starts pacing back and forth.)* Can any government that admits vigorous execution be established on republican principles? No, gentlemen. The English model is the only good one on this subject. Let one branch of the legislature hold their places for life, or at least during good behavior. And let the executive *also* be for life. Let him have such power that it will not be in his interest to acquire more.

FRANKLIN *(turns to look up at Hamilton)*: Hold it right there, sir. What you're proposing is a *monarch!*

HAMILTON: What our government needs is a principle capable of resisting the popular current. What it needs is an impartial arbiter to transcend differences of region and class. What it needs is a check, and that check *is* a monarch.

FRANKLIN: I'm sorry, sir, that won't do. That is precisely what we fought against in the Revolution.

MORRIS: Even for me, my friend, your proposal goes too far.

HAMILTON: Well then, since I have no wish to suffer through further debate on Mr. Madison's plan I shall take my leave. Good day, gentlemen. *(All eyes follow Hamilton as he exits)*

MODERATOR: Well, that was...interesting.

MADISON: Mr. Hamilton could be out of his wits at times.

MODERATOR: Weren't you upset that he rejected your plan?

MADISON: No. I knew at once the House would see mine in a more benign light.

FRANKLIN *(to the moderator)*: You do know about Mr. Hamilton's childhood, don't you?

MODERATOR: He told us about it earlier.

FRANKLIN: Well, I have a theory about why he wanted a monarch.

MODERATOR: What is it?

FRANKLIN: As a boy Mr. Hamilton never had a father, an

authority figure, to look up to. It was a void throughout his childhood. As an adult he still needed someone to fill that void—someone like General Washington. *(He turns to the others.)* Don't you see, gentlemen, how he transferred his need for authority from his private life to his public life?

MODERATOR: You sound like a psychologist, Dr. Franklin.

FRANKLIN: I beg your pardon. I sound like a what?

MODERATOR: A psychologist, one who studies how the mind works.

FRANKLIN: I don't believe I'm familiar with the term. *(George Washington, resplendent in his general's uniform, enters unannounced, brandishing a sheet of paper.)*

WASHINGTON: Gentlemen! *(Everyone instinctively rises; Morris does so somewhat unsteadily. The moderator withdraws while the scene plays out in real time.)*

MADISON: General Washington—good day, sir.

FRANKLIN: Welcome, sir.

MORRIS *(staggers over to Washington and cuffs his shoulder)*: My dear general, what a surprise to see you, and how happy I am to see you look so well! *(Washington fixes Morris with an icy gaze and Morris retreats.)*

WASHINGTON: Gentlemen, I'm sorry to find that a member of this body has been so neglectful of the secrecy of the convention as to drop a copy of our proceedings on the floor. *(Holds up the sheet of paper.)* This was picked up and delivered to me this morning. *(The others steal glances from their colleagues and shake their heads in denial.)* I must entreat you, gentlemen, to be more careful lest our transactions get into the newspapers and disturb the public repose. I don't know whose paper this is *(he drops it on the table)*, but here it is. Let him who owns it take it. By the way, where is Colonel Hamilton?

MADISON: He took his leave early, sir. He grew impatient with our deliberations.

WASHINGTON: I am sorry he left. I despair myself of seeing

a favorable issue to the convention and therefore repent of having any agency in this business. Whatever the result, I doubt the new federal government will survive twenty years. Well, carry on, gentlemen and do the best you can. The fate of America is in your hands. *(Exits)*

MADISON: Aye, sir.

MORRIS *(sheepishly)*: Aye.

FRANKLIN *(to Morris, with a chuckle)*: Well, Gouv, it looks like you won your wager.

MORRIS *(shrinks into his chair):* May I die a thousand deaths!

FRANKLIN: Gentlemen, we still have the representation issue to settle. Our differences on that question are the chief obstacle to our reaching agreement. With proportional representation, the small states fear their *liberties* will be in danger. With equality of votes, the larger states fear their *money* will be in danger. We must find a compromise, gentlemen, or we will fail in our mission.

MORRIS: How do you propose we do that?

FRANKLIN: Sometimes we must abandon a small bit of our ideas so we may unite the whole. When a cabinet maker makes a table out of two planks and they don't exactly fit, he takes a small bit from each in order to join them together. In like manner, both sides must part with some of their demands in order to join in some accommodating proposition. I propose, therefore, that a committee be appointed to break the impasse.

MADISON: With due respect, sir, I think we should proceed with debate.

FRANKLIN *(taps his cane on the floor)*: Please hear me out, gentlemen. We are sent hither to *consult*, not to *contend*, with each other. I sense the intransigence on both sides is beginning to ease. Let it ease further through thoughtful reflection rather than through declamations and denouncements. And let it be done by honorable gentlemen from both sides who declare to have in common the common good. Furthermore, gentlemen, tomorrow is the Fourth of July. It was on this date, eleven years ago, that I gave my assent to the

Declaration of Independence. The time is nigh for us to establish a government that will prove to the world that we can indeed make it on our own. *(Franklin turns to the moderator.)* That, sir, is what I told the delegates on the eve of the Fourth of July, 1787, the eleventh year of our Independence.

MODERATOR: What happened after that?

FRANKLIN: The president appointed a committee of eleven. For the next two days, while the rest of us celebrated the anniversary of Independence, they worked out a compromise proposed by Roger Sherman of Connecticut. His plan called for a House of Representatives elected on the basis of population and a Senate in which each state would have an equal vote. After several more weeks of give and take the House voted to adopt Mr. Sherman's plan.

MODERATOR: Today we call it the Great Compromise.

FRANKLIN: Is that so? Well, it was indeed a compromise, but it was only through compromise that we were able to break the impasse. By taking a small bit from each plank, we were able to keep the table from collapsing.

MODERATOR: It's a lesson for our time. *(Hamilton enters)*

MADISON: Well, Mr. Hamilton is back! *(The scene shifts back to real time.)*

HAMILTON: I changed my mind, gentlemen. When I learned of Mr. Sherman's compromise it restored my faith that we would succeed in this endeavor.

FRANKLIN: Gentlemen, I don't wish to dim your enthusiasm, but we have another obstacle to overcome: that is how to put an end to the insidious institution of slavery. The southern colonies say if we continue to debate the issue they will walk out. What then?

MADISON: We must do the best we can as General Washington said. What has been proposed is that the importation of slaves be prohibited, but not until the year 1808.

FRANKLIN: That's not what I would choose, not at all. Nor

would I choose as the basis for apportionment in the lower house the whole number of *free* persons and three-fifths of persons *bound to service.* Does that mean a slave is to be considered three-fifths of a person? No, gentlemen, this goes against the very fiber of my being. But...one must take what is in one's hands and bless it.

HAMILTON: What happened to my proposal regarding the chief executive?

MADISON: Oh, *that.* Well, another committee was appointed to look into it. They decided that a *president* would be chosen every four years by electors from each state and that the number of electors from each state would be equal to the number of its representatives in Congress. Think of it as an electoral *(searches for the right word)...* college.

HAMILTON: An electorial what?

MADISON: An electorial college.

HAMILTON *(pauses, turns to the audience)*: That is the dumbest thing I ever heard!

FRANKLIN: But once again, gentlemen, one must take what one can get...through compromise. *(Franklin turns to the moderator.)* That, my friend, is what happened.

MODERATOR: That was it?

FRANKLIN: Oh no. Another committee was appointed.

MODERATOR: *Another* committee?

FRANKLIN: Another committee. Mr. Madison, suppose you explain to the gentleman.

MADISON: It was called the Committee of Style and Arrangement. I was appointed to it along with Mr. Morris and Mr. Hamilton. Our task was to produce a final draft of the Constitution. After consulting among ourselves we picked Mr. Morris to write it. He alone in our opinion had the ability to "clothe the skeleton in muscles"—as he put it—with the grace and dignity required of such a document. *(Looks over to Morris who has dozed off)* Mr. Morris? Mr. Morris? *(The moderator withdraws as the scene shifts into real time.)*

MORRIS *(startled)*: Yes?

MADISON: Would you read what you wrote for the preamble, please?

MORRIS: The preamble?

MADISON: Just the preamble

MORRIS *(rolls out the scroll, steadies himself, and reads)*: "We the People of the United States, in Order to form a more perfect Union, establish Justice, insure domestic Tranquility, provide for the common defense, promote the general Welfare, and secure the Blessings of Liberty to ourselves and our Posterity, do ordain and establish this Constitution for the United States of America."

HAMILTON: Sometimes you do amaze me, my friend!

FRANKLIN: I wish I had written it myself.

MORRIS *(to Franklin)*: Then would you sign right here, please? *(He reaches for the quill and hands it to Franklin.)*

FRANKLIN *(holding the quill)*: I confess, gentlemen, that I do not approve of several parts of this constitution, but I'm not sure that I shall *never* approve them. For having lived long, I have often found instances of being obliged by better information. The older I get, the more apt I am to doubt my own judgment and pay more respect to the judgment of others. Therefore, gentlemen, I agree to this constitution with all its faults, because I expect no better, and because I'm not sure it is not the best. *(He signs the document and passes it on to Hamilton)*.

HAMILTON: No man's ideas are more remote from this document than mine. (*He sighs.)* Nevertheless, it's better than nothing. *(He signs and passes it to Madison.)*

MADISON: Better than nothing? This document will do nothing less than decide forever the fate of republican government. *(Madison signs and passes the document back to Morris who signs and holds it up for all to see.)*

FRANKLIN: For four months, gentlemen, I have looked up at the president's chair and observed a carving of the sun with outstretched rays.

I couldn't tell whether it was a rising sun or a setting sun. But now I have the happiness to know that it's a rising sun.

MADISON: If I may say so, gentlemen, the union of so many states is, in the eyes of the world, a wonder.

FRANKLIN: The wonder, gentlemen, is that our union is not a monarchy, but a republic—if we can keep it.

MODERATOR *(facing the audience)*: And so, on September 17, 1787, the delegates finished their work. Today we call it the "miracle at Philadelphia." Nobody thought that this new American republic, this bold experiment in self-government, would last. It has, longer than any other republic in the world. Still, we might ask ourselves once in a while as old, wise Ben Franklin did when it all started: Can we keep it?

Now on behalf of President James Madison, Mr. Alexander Hamilton, Dr. Benjamin Franklin, Mr. Gouverneur Morris, and the Father of our Country, General George Washington, thank you and God bless.

EPISODE 3

Liberty for All

The Untold Story of the Bill of Rights

STAGING NOTE

The stage should be set with four chairs and a moderator's podium. Halfway through the program, the moderator transitions from a talk show format to a town hall meeting in which the actors playing James Madison, Thomas Jefferson, Alexander Hamilton and Patrick Henry take questions from the audience. Their answers are improvised but generally reflect the Founders' views. Students are encouraged to do the same by applying the Founders' ideas to the 21st century. What would the Founders say, for example, about same-sex marriage? Gun control? Abortion? Capital punishment? Corporate financing of political campaigns? Electronic surveillance of private citizens?

CAST OF CHARACTERS

THOMAS JEFFERSON (1743-1826). Champion of the Bill of Rights. While conspicuously absent from the Constitutional Convention and the ratification debates (he was Minister to France at the time), he nagged James Madison and others from across the Atlantic on the need to add a bill of rights to the Constitution.

JAMES MADISON (1751-1836). Father of the Constitution. Slight-of-build, high-strung and persnickety, he worked harder than any other Founder to frame a government for the new nation. Then, with Alexander Hamilton, he helped sell it to the American people. While initially opposed to adding a bill of rights, he eventually became its author.

ALEXANDER HAMILTON (1755?-1804). Principal author of the Federalist Papers. While disappointed in the outcome of the Constitutional Convention—he had in fact proposed a monarchy on the British model—he became with James Madison the Constitution's most articulate spokesperson. Only recently has history given him his due.

PATRICK HENRY (1736-1799). Orator of the Revolution. While his fiery speeches stirred his fellow Virginians to rebel against the British, he stubbornly resisted a federal constitution. Next to his "Liberty or Death" speech calling for arms, his "We the People, We the States" speech opposing ratification is perhaps his best remembered.

EPISODE 3

Liberty For All

MODERATOR: Welcome to Episode 3 of *Inventing America*. In the first episode, we talked about how the thirteen American colonies declared their independence from Great Britain. In the second episode, we talked about how our founders created a new constitution for an infant nation. But what they created—what we think of today as the "Miracle at Philadelphia"—was anything but that at the beginning. Many of the founders adamantly opposed it. Why? Well, tonight we'll find out. And we'll find out why they changed their minds. Each of our guests played a critical role in making that happen. More than two centuries later, the solution they came up with not only defines who we are as Americans but serves as a beacon of liberty to the world.

Our first guest is from the State of Virginia. We remember him not only as the fourth President of the United States but also as the Father of our Constitution. Please welcome Mr. James Madison. *(Madison enters carrying a satchel and shakes Fred's hand.)* It's an honor to have you back, sir.

MADISON: Well, it wasn't easy.

MODERATOR: I don't understand.

MADISON: I was in frail health my whole life. Imagine how I feel now.

MODERATOR: All the more reason we're glad to have you back. And I think you'll be happy to meet your old mentor, Mr. Jefferson.

MADISON: You mean he's joining us?

MODERATOR: Indeed, he is. *(Turns to the audience)* We're also pleased to have back on the program the author of the Declaration of Independence and Mr. Madison's predecessor as president—today we think of him as America's foremost champion of human rights—Mr. Thomas Jefferson. *(Jefferson enters, bypasses the moderator, goes straight to Madison and shakes his hand vigorously.*

JEFFERSON: My dear Madison, how good it is to see you! *(Madison bows as he shakes Jefferson's hand.)* If I may say so, you look better than the last time I saw you.

MADISON: Thank you, sir.

JEFFERSON *(turns to the moderator and shakes his hand)*: And it is good to see you again, sir.

MODERATOR: Thank you, Mr. President. But I'm not so sure you will be happy to meet our next guest –

JEFFERSON: Oh?

MODERATOR: –because the two of you ended up as political rivals.

JEFFERSON: Good lord, that could be most anyone!

MODERATOR: I'm speaking of Mr. Hamilton.

JEFFERSON: Oh, well.

MODERATOR *(to the audience)*: Our next guest has only recently found his place in history. He served our country in many ways, first as General Washington's aide-de-camp during the Revolution and later as our nation's first Secretary of the Treasury. But tonight we remember him as an ardent defender of the Constitution. Please welcome Mr. Alexander Hamilton. *(Hamilton enters and shakes moderator's hand, then Madison's, then, somewhat haltingly, Jefferson's.)*

MODERATOR: It's an honor to have you back, sir.

HAMILTON: Thank you. The honor is mine. But I should point out that until we served on President Washington's cabinet—Mr. Jefferson as secretary of state and yours truly as secretary of the treasury—we were allies in the cause of liberty.

JEFFERSON: Indeed, we were. Only later did we become rivals.

MODERATOR *(turns to the audience)*: Speaking of liberty, we remember our next guest as the Orator of the Revolution. He was in fact a planter and a lawyer by occupation. After the Revolution, he served as the first governor of post-colonial Virginia. Please welcome Mr. Patrick Henry. (*Henry enters and shakes the moderator's hand, then shakes the others' hands.)*

MODERATOR: Please have a seat, gentlemen. *(To Hamilton, Madison and Jefferson)* Once again, it's an honor to have you back. *(To Henry)* And Mr. Henry, sir, it's an honor to have you on the program for the first time.

HENRY: I thought you'd never ask.

MODERATOR: Isn't it true, sir, that after you roused your fellow Virginians to rebel against the British—I think of your famous "Give me liberty, or give me death" speech—that you would have nothing to do with a new federal constitution?

HENRY: That is correct. The reason I objected—

MADISON *(interrupting):* The reason you objected, sir, is that any jackass can kick down a barn. It takes a skilled carpenter to build one.

HENRY *(annoyed):* Sir, the reason I objected is that it put too much power at the top. It endangered not only the rights of the states but the freedoms of individual citizens.

MADISON *(to Henry):* What about the slaves your wife's father gave you on your wedding day?

HENRY: Slaves were not citizens. As a slaveowner yourself, you should know—

MODERATOR: Please, gentlemen, we just started. Mr. Henry, tell me something about yourself. We remember you for your "Liberty-or-Death" speech but not much else.

HENRY *(mildly offended)*: Is that so! Well, I was born on a plantation in Virginia. When my wife and I married, her father gave us six slaves – Mr. Madison is correct about that – and some land on which we tried to grow tobacco. But the crops failed and then our house burned down.

MODERATOR: You weren't cut out to be a farmer it seems.

HENRY: Then I opened a mercantile store and that failed. After that my wife had a mental breakdown and died. She left me with six children.

MODERATOR: Six children!

HENRY: More came after I married my second wife. Her name was Dorothea Dandridge. She was 22. I was 41. We had eleven more children and seventy-seven grandchildren. Yes, father of his country indeed. Meanwhile I had taken up politics.

MODERATOR: Sounds like you had a good voter base.

HENRY: Before that I had taken up the reading of law. After six weeks – six weeks, mind you – I passed the Virginia bar exam and became a lawyer. In 1763, I won my first important case. It was called the Parson's Cause. It determined whether the price of tobacco paid to clergy for their ecclesiastical services should be set by local authorities or the Crown. It turned out I was better at *litigating* tobacco than growing it.

MODERATOR: When did you take up politics?

HENRY: In 1765, when Parliament passed the Stamp Act. I had just been elected to the House of Burgesses, our legislative assembly in Williamsburg, when I gave my first political speech.

JEFFERSON: I remember eavesdropping at the door.

HENRY: "Caesar had his Brutus...," I said, "Charles the First his Cromwell, and George the Third..."

JEFFERSON: Then I heard somebody shout "Treason!"

HENRY: "...and George the Third," I said, "...may he profit by their example."

MODERATOR: It must have been a remarkable a speech.

HENRY *(proudly)*: The first of many, if I may say so, in my public life.

MODERATOR: So, Mr. Jefferson, you heard Mr. Henry's speech.

JEFFERSON: Indeed, I did. I was twenty-two at the time, reading the law under Mr. George Wythe in Williamsburg. I remember how awestruck I was. But in due course I came to wonder how Mr. Henry acquired his way with words because he was the laziest man for reading I ever knew.

HENRY: Mr. Jefferson, it took you four years, did it not, to pass the bar exam? As I said, it took me six weeks. Do I detect a hint of jealousy?

MODERATOR: Please, gentlemen, let's keep this civil. I want to get Mr. Hamilton in on the discussion. Sir, you never met Mr. Henry in real life, is that correct?

HAMILTON: That is correct. But distance played a big part in that.

MADISON: Political as well as geographical.

HAMILTON: Yes, I would agree with that. We were at opposite ends of the political spectrum.

MODERATOR: Can you explain?

HAMILTON: I led the so-called Federalist movement in support of the Constitution. Mr. Henry led the Anti-Federalist movement in opposition to it. He opposed having a Constitutional Convention in the first place.

MADISON *(to Henry):* Tell the gentleman what you said when you learned about it.

HENRY *(to the moderator):* I said I smelt a rat.

MODERATOR *(to Hamilton):* But if I recall, sir, you weren't very pleased with the outcome yourself.

HAMILTON: I wasn't. No man's ideas were more remote from the Constitution than mine.

MODERATOR: So what made you change your mind?

HAMILTON: Doctor Franklin, may he rest in peace. Or more precisely, the words he spoke when we finished our work.

MODERATOR: What did he say?

HAMILTON: That the older he got, the more he doubted his own judgment and paid respect to the judgment of others.

MODERATOR: We could benefit from his wisdom today.

HAMILTON: I also came to the conclusion, as did Dr. Franklin, that we could do no better; that the Constitution, with all its faults, was the best any assembly of mortals could do.

JEFFERSON *(aside)*: Notwithstanding an assembly of demigods.

HAMILTON: So we set about the task of getting it ratified.

MADISON: That required approval of nine of the thirteen states. It was up to each state to ratify it. You remember how the preamble reads: "We the people of the United States…."

MODERATOR: Yes, "We the people."

MADISON: At issue was who had the power to govern? The people or the states? That was our single most divisive issue.

HAMILTON: To answer that question, and many others that came up in the ratification debates, I wrote a series of essays with the help of Mr. Madison and Mr. John Jay of New York. These essays were first published in newspapers and later assembled into a volume called *The Federalist.*

JEFFERSON: Yes, Mr. Madison sent me a copy. I have it here. *(produces a copy)* It is the best commentary on the principles of government that ever was written.

HAMILTON: Between the three of us, we wrote 85 essays in ten months. I wrote 51 of them myself.

MODERATOR: Can you cite some of the arguments you made? Mr. Madison too, if you don't mind. *(Jefferson hands his copy to Madison, who passes it along to Hamilton)*

HAMILTON: In Federalist No. 1 – we assigned a number to each essay – I wrote the following: "It (has been) reserved to the people of this country, by their conduct and example, to decide the important question, whether societies of men are capable of establishing good government from reflection and choice, or whether they are forever destined to depend on accident or force."

MADSON: In Federalist 10 I argued against rule by majority faction.

HAMILTON: In Federalist 70 I argued for a one-man chief executive. *(Hands Jefferson's copy back to Madison)*

MADISON: In Federalist 51 I argued for checks and balances between the three branches of government – the legislative, the executive and the judicial. I also observed that government was the greatest reflection on human nature. *(Hands Jefferson's copy back to him)*

MODERATOR: Now, Mr. Jefferson, if I'm not mistaken, sir, you were in Paris during the Convention and ratification debates.

JEFFERSON: That is correct. You do know your history.

MODERATOR: And isn't it correct, sir, that you had replaced Dr. Franklin as Minister to France?

JEFFERSON: Not quite. I did not replace him. I *succeeded* him. Dr. Franklin could never be replaced.

MODERATOR: Well, I do stand corrected on that.

JEFFERSON: We owed much to the French for helping us gain our independence from England – remember they gave us the Marquis de Lafayette – but it wasn't the same country when I took up my post in 1784. The indignities and assaults on personal liberties that led to the French Revolution were in many ways a repeat of the abuses that led to our own revolution. I had seen it all before.

MODERATOR: We call that *déjà vu.*

JEFFERSON: So, you know a little French, too! Well, there were similarities—and some differences. In Boston, Americans threw tea into the harbor. In Paris, the French stormed the Bastille. I saw it happen. Oh, what date was that?

MODERATOR: Bastille Day is July 14.

JEFFERSON: That is correct, sir! The 14th of July, 1789. On that day, I witnessed firsthand the outbreak of French Revolution. We all know what that led to.

MODERATOR: Louis XVI and Marie Antionette would be no more.

JEFFERSON: And that was the end of monarchy in France. That impressed upon me the need to add a bill of rights to the constitution that Mr. Madison and Mr. Hamilton and others had hammered out back in Philadelphia – a list of guarantees of individual liberties that government could not infringe upon.

MADISON: At first, I objected to Mr. Jefferson's proposal.

MODERATOR: Why so?

MADISON: I believed that state governments were sufficient guarantors of personal liberties.

HAMILTON: I didn't support Mr. Jefferson's proposal either. In Federalist No. 84 I argued that such guarantees were already inherent in the new Constitution.

MADISON: What it boiled down to was that by the end of the Convention we were too worn out to take up debate on a bill of rights. We left it to fate – providence if you will – as to how that would play out.

MODERATOR: So?

MADISON: It turned into a colossal mistake. Whether or not to add a bill of rights became the most contentious issue in the ratification debates. In Massachusetts, at their ratifying convention, a fistfight broke out. It didn't go much better in my own state, Virginia. Before the Constitution came to a vote Mr. Henry rose in opposition and launched into another one of his demagogic rants.

MODERATOR: Take us back to that moment.

MADISON: We met in convention in Richmond on the 2nd of June, 1788. By then, eight of the thirteen states – one short of the two thirds needed – had already ratified the Constitution. This meant that Virginia's vote was critical. On the third day of the convention, Mr. Henry took the floor.

HENRY *(in flashback)*: "Gentlemen, whither is the spirit of America gone? Whither is the genius of America fled? We drew the spirit of liberty from our British ancestors. But now, gentlemen, the American spirit, assisted by the ropes and chains of consolidation, is about to convert this country into a powerful and mighty empire. Will there be no checks or balances in this government? What can avail your specious, imaginary balances, your rope-dancing, chain-rattling, ridiculous ideal checks and contrivances? I would make this inquiry of those who composed the late federal Convention: What right had they to say, *We, the people*? Who authorized them to speak the language of *We, the people*, instead of *We, the states*? The people gave them no power to use their name. The states are the soul of our confederation. May they remain so." *(Henry bows with a flourish and resumes his seat)*

MODERATOR: Thank you, Mr. Henry. So, Mr. Madison, how did the vote go after that?

MADISON: In spite of Mr. Henry's plea, we voted to ratify the Constitution – 89 in favor, 79 against – along with a bill of rights. Even with that, Mr. Henry wasn't very happy.

MODERATOR: Tell me about the Bill of Rights.

MADISON: Well, we intended them as amendments to the Constitution. We started out with seventeen. We ended up with ten. Without Mr. Jefferson pestering us from France we probably would have ended up with none, or with no Constitution at all.

MODERATOR: Can you read some of them to us?

MADISON: *(removes a parchment copy of the Constitution from his satchel, rolls it out and reads)*: "One. Congress shall make no law respecting an establishment of religion...or abridging the freedom of speech, or of the press; or of the right of the people to peaceably assemble. Two. A well-regulated Militia being necessary to the security of a free State, the right of the people to keep and bear Arms shall not be infringed. Three. No Soldier shall, in time of peace, be quartered in any house, without the consent of the Owner. Four. The right of people to be secure... against unreasonable searches and seizures, shall not be violated. Five. No person shall be... compelled in any criminal case to be a witness against himself. Eight. Excessive bail shall not be required...nor cruel and unusual punishments inflicted. Ten. The powers not delegated to the United States by the Constitution, or prohibited to it by the States, are reserved to the States respectively, or to the people."

MODERATOR (*to Madison)*: Sir, it occurred to me as you were reading that it might not be a bad idea if the President were required on Inauguration Day not to give a speech but instead stand before the Chief Justice of the United States and recite the Bill of Rights.

JEFFERSON: If I may say so that is a splendid idea, but I was never fond of making speeches.

HENRY: As for me, I would rather make a speech.

MODERATOR *(to Madison)*: Sir, the last time you were on this program you spoke of George Mason and the Virginia Declaration of Rights. How much did that influence the Bill of Rights in the U.S. Constitution?

MADISON: A great deal. But it wasn't the only influence. The ideas go back to the Magna Carta and the English Bill of Rights that Parliament passed in 1689. It even guaranteed the right to keep and bear arms, although the right applied only to Protestants.

MODERATOR: Not to Catholics?

MADISON: You can blame that on Henry VIII. If you remember, he wasn't very fond of Catholics. But we did improve upon the English version.

MODERATOR: When was the Constitution ratified?

MADISON: The 21st of June, 1788. New Hampshire was the ninth state to ratify.

MODERATOR: And the Bill of Rights?

MADISON: The 15th of December, 1791, two years and eight months after George Washington was inaugurated.

MODERATOR: December 15, Bill of Rights Day. Thank you, gentlemen. *(He faces the audience.)* Of the four-and-a-half thousand words of the U.S. Constitution, the most hotly debated are the four hundred and sixty-two that that comprise the first ten amendments, the Bill of Rights. Whether the issue be freedom of speech or freedom of assembly, the right to bear arms or any of the other freedoms spelled out in those amendments, it's that part of the Constitution that we the *people* of the United States most often look to the *Supreme Court* of the United States to decide how they apply to us. In the next part of our program we're going to find out what the Founding Fathers have to say about that. What did they have in mind when they wrote the Bill of Rights? What was their intent? What wisdom do they have for us in the 21st century? Let's find out what they have to say to us today.

QUESTIONER #1: My question is for Mr. Hamilton. You said you objected to the Bill of Rights because such guarantees were already inherent in the Constitution. Why not spell them out?

HAMILTON: I appreciate your question for several reasons. First, it is an important one. It also allows me to set some distance between myself and *(gesturing to the others)* three members of what I call the Virginia Junta. I will say this as clearly as I can: a bill of rights is a foolish and dangerous idea. Note the word. I do not say that *rights* are foolish, but a *bill* of rights. There are several reasons for this. First, I am told that in your day you do not use the mathematics of our day to calculate the building of your skyscrapers. You do not use the medicinc of our day to treat your children's illnesses. Yet you somehow cling to the notion that the only political wisdom possible comes from a world in which information can travel no faster than a galloping horse or a ship at sea. There is a danger of locking your concept of rights into an era that no longer applies. I am told that in your day you revere your first and second amendments, but how many of you spend much time thinking about your third? How many of you worry about the notion that British soldiers will be forced into your home against your will? I want you to imagine a time in our nation when perhaps an individual is elected to high office who is both ignorant and a tyrant, a person who would quest after power and might look at a bill of rights and say, ah, these are your rights, these your *only* rights. I see that it says you have freedom of speech. It says nothing about freedom of protest songs. It says you have freedom of the press. The press is a printing press. So your television news is not protected. When you list rights you create a profound danger that a future demagogue could say that these are the only rights you have. And that is a risk not worth taking in any century.

JEFFERSON *(to Hamilton):* I beg your pardon, sir. Indeed, a bill of rights ought not to be inferred in our Constitution, because we do not know precisely what they may become in the future any less than what they were in the past. Are we to rest upon inference upon such an important subject as the inherent rights of man? Are they to be any different in the future than they have been in the past? Have they not existed from time in memoriam, and are they not given to mankind not by any government, not by any ruler, but given to mankind by nature and nature's God?

HAMILTON: No, sir. Fundamental rights, as I wrote, are not to be rummaged for among ancient parchments or dusty records. They are written like a sunbeam upon the whole volume of human nature, and no mortal power can erase or obscure them. You have fundamental, natural rights. But what those rights might mean in any given era must rely on the wisdom of the people, sir, that you revere with such greatness.

JEFFERSON: I beg your pardon, sir. We're talking about the inalienable rights from time in memoriam, the inalienable rights of man. It is not the duty of government to *infer* these rights any more than it is the duty of government to try to change human nature.

HAMILTON: If government, sir, represents the people, then the people must decide in any given era what, for example, the concept of free speech means.

JEFFERSON: Then have faith in the people, sir. Do not have fear. And remind yourself that we are free to declare and therefore we must declare that these are the inalienable rights of man.

QUESTIONER #2: My question is for Mr. Jefferson. Recently in your hometown of Charlottesville, Virginia, one person was killed and many others were injured at a so-called free speech demonstration. Aren't there times like this when First Amendment guarantees of freedom of speech and freedom of assembly go too far?

JEFFERSON: I have heard of what transpired in my native town as I was making my way westward. I am quite dismayed and upset that such a liberty protected by the First Amendment can be taken so far as to inflict hostility and aggression upon our citizens. Is it not the purpose of our Constitution, as pronounced in the Preamble, to maintain not only the public welfare but the public peace? I would agree that if any of our amendments guaranteeing inalienable rights are wont to go too far as to inflict hostility, to inflict aggression upon the people, well then, the people ought to let their opinion be heard rather than to lose those rights. Yes, it is the first and foremost inalienable right to hold an opinion freely and to freely express one's opinion but not to go so far as to inflict harm or death upon an individual. That is not a right. That, if you will, is an oppression. It is a crime.

HAMILTON *(to Jefferson):* You seem to suggest, sir, that rights, though fundamental, may need to be altered by the time and era in which the event takes place.

JEFFERSON: I am saying that if a right goes too far, then it must be attended to with the law.

HENRY: Hear, hear! How about that. Jefferson and I agree!

HAMILTON: You're both wrong.

QUESTIONER #3: My question is for Mr. Madison. It has to do with the Second Amendment, the right to keep and bear arms. Since militias, well-regulated or otherwise, are no longer necessary to the security of a free state, isn't that amendment obsolete? Why not repeal it?

MADISON: Thank you for the question. When we sought to form a republican government in Philadelphia in 1787, we were concerned that it would not intrude upon the rights of individuals. There was no authority granted to the Constitution that would in any way allow it to intrude upon such rights of individuals, rights that were extant before the Constitution was written, even before our Declaration of Independence, even before the first breath of mankind. If these rights were extant before a government was formed, it seemed only reasonable that you would form a government that did not abridge those rights. What we were seeking to do was not to enumerate those rights, but to phrase them in such a way as to limit the government's authority. When a government is formed, should not the very rights we have in nature carry the same weight in community? Your question refers to rendering the Second Amendment obsolete. Why not repeal it? I suggest we should not consider repealing those rights which were extant before we formed a government.

MODERATOR: While we're on the Second Amendment, I would like to ask a question of Patrick Henry. Sir, if you consider the right to keep and bear arms in the context of the 18th century, wasn't that a military expression? One might bear arms against an enemy of the state but not, say, against a rabbit or your next-door neighbor. I know that you were adamant in your day about the right to keep and bear arms. But did you intend that right to extend from military life to civilian life?

HENRY: Thank you for your question. I have said many times that I have been a devoted student on the subject of history, because that way I know where I am and where I am likely to go. In 1622, only fifteen years after English feet touched Virginia soil, there was an uprising of the Pamunkey Nation, the Indians in that part of the country. Nearly half of the entire British population was massacred. Ever since that time we have had militia laws in place requiring all able-bodied males above the age of eighteen to own a gun, one pound of gunpowder, four pounds of shot. They are required to muster three to seven times each year to reacquaint themselves with the manual of arms and to practice the military exercise. This is our militia system, our citizens army. And the understanding has always been that the citizens army, by every male being armed, would be stronger and thus be able to defeat any invasion or any standing army raised up by a government that might become oppressive. So certainly, in our tradition in Virginia, the right to keep and bear arms has a military element to it. However, we must also pay attention to the great philosopher John Locke, whom many regard as the greatest genius of the Enlightened Age, who assured us that rights come from God, not from government, and that such rights pertain to life, liberty and property. And naturally with that right goes the protection and defense of same. Thus, the right to keep and bear arms is also an individual right which must never be infringed. As I stated back in 1775, never trust that government that seeks to remove your arms, for there can be but one purpose to it and one alone: to remove your means of self-defense, thereby making an easy conquest of you, and to fasten more tightly to your wrists the shackles of slavery.

HAMILTON: Colonel Henry with his great eloquence proves my point. I think you would agree, Mr. Madison, that the intent of the Second Amendment is to assure that the citizenry would have sufficient weaponry to overthrow a government should it become tyrannical.

MADISON: In part.

HAMILTON: In great danger, sir. *(Turns to the audience.)* In your day do you wish your citizens to be armed in such a way as to take down the United States Army? Do you want your unusual neighbor to have access to an anthrax cannon, or your strange uncle that you see only at Christmas to have a flame thrower? To lock these rights in time creates dangers in yours.

QUESTIONNER #4: Mr. Madison, today in the 21st century we have devices called cell phones. Imagine a speaking trumpet that allows you to contact anyone on earth at any time, any place. My question is, should the Fourth Amendment's ban on unreasonable searches require a warrant for police to acquire records of a cell phone? This question is now before the Supreme Court.

MADISON: Once again, we should not forget rights that are extant in our nation and that amongst them is the protection against unreasonable searches and seizures. Each generation engages with its own time and place. That you even bring the question to the fore indicates that there is a concern about the application of the right to a particular circumstance. How do you feel about the answer, sir?

QUESTIONNER: Personally, I don't want any police officers looking at my cell phone, let alone my parents.

MADISON: You don't want a police officer looking at your parents?

QUESTIONNER: I guess not. It's a complicated issue and I'm looking forward to the Supreme Court's decision.

MADISON: Well, I can only add in matter of advice by age and capacity that even though there seems to be an evolving of the decision upon the Supreme Court of the United States, that not one of us would consider any decision of the court, however elevated in matters of jurisprudence, to be the end of the answer. If collective society feels in this instance that search and seizure is unreasonable, they have the capacity as citizens of the country, as citizens of their respective states, to invite an amendment to the Constitution that may contradict the assertion of the Supreme Court.

QUESTIONNER #5: Mr. Jefferson, in today's political discourse we hear a lot about walls, walls that separate us. You yourself called for a wall of separation between church and state. Yet, starting in your time and continuing to our own, a chaplain opens each session of Congress with prayer. Indeed, our currency, whether it's a quarter or a $10 bill, bears the inscription, "In God we trust." Aren't these things in violation of the First Amendment that states, "Congress shall make no law respecting an establishment of religion?"

JEFFERSON: I beg your pardon, did you say that our currency, the specie of our nation, bears the inscription, "In God we Trust?"

QUESTIONNER: "In God we trust."

JEFFERSON: I do declare, Mr. Hamilton, we collaborated, did we not, upon standardizing our nation's currency, to make it the same value in Georgia and the Carolinas as in Virginia, Massachusetts, Rhode Island and the Providence Plantations? To think that we established a national mint, and then to have our specie with such a statement stamped upon it? I do believe that is a heresy. It must be unto our creator. Would not all Christians have forgotten the reason Jesus threw the money lenders out of the temple? Unto what are we providing now: an allegiance, a recognition of our creator, with money?

Yes, I did make a statement about a separation, a wall, a great wall of separation between church and state. I did not proffer it publicly. I provided it in an answer to a letter I received from a coterie of Baptist ministers in Danbury, Connecticut. They wrote me during my first administration asking my opinion upon the fact that in Connecticut they had to abide by the constitution of their state to continue to offer a tithing, money to support the Congregational Church. They asked me if our federal constitution did not supersede that. After all, it was the law of the land. I wrote back to them and said, "Bear with patience until the constitution of Connecticut amends itself to the constitution of our nation." And yes, no one more than myself would rather see a great wall of separation be built between church and state.

I ask you, citizens, is it the duty of government to dictate religious opinion? I dare say the reason so many of you and your ancestors sought asylum here was to escape those ancient tumults and calumnies of European kingdoms that coerced their subjects to attend one religion more than another, to furnish contributions of money to one religion more than another. No, the only duty of any government and its laws is simply to protect people from injury by one and another. Otherwise to leave them free, to pursue their own industry and their own improvement, and their improvement will be the most successful when the ecclesiastical laws are free to attend to their duty: the administration of the soul in an effort simply to do good.

QUESTIONNER #6: My question is for Mr. Hamilton. I direct this to you because of your connection to Wall Street. Recently the Supreme Court ruled that corporations have the same free speech rights as individuals and thus can make unlimited political contributions. Do you agree with that?

HAMILTON: Thank you for your question. I would add to that I did have an office on Wall Street and was engaged in a number of monetary affairs. The question earlier reminded me that my visage is upon your $10 bill, Mr. Jefferson's upon your nickel.

JEFFERSON: And may I remind you, sir, that there are far more nickels than $10 bills. You're speechless, I see.

HAMILTON: I am rarely speechless, sir. But to the question, which

I will answer in two parts. First, as to whether a corporation can have the same rights as a person: The answer is a legal one. It is trivially true, yes, corporations can have some of the rights as people. A college can own this building. A grocery story can own the parking lot in which you park your conveyances. These are trivial notions of personhood that corporations share. But the larger question I believe you're asking is about their role in politics. I will say this: I wrote of Mr. Jefferson that he most ardently quested after the presidential chair, in spite of denials of any such interest. Yet Mr. Jefferson in pursuit of that office would never dream of leaving his own front porch. It would be undignified to campaign. I am told that you are now in a different era. And so, given that we lived in a three-mile-per-hour world, I am reluctant to tell you what to do in your campaign today. But I would point out that we gave you a provision in the Constitution to deal with this very issue. In Article I, Section 4, it states clearly that the states shall have the right to decide the time, the place and the manner of elections. And I would certainly think that that the funding of elections, the way in which elections are conducted, would fall under the notion of "manner." So, in your day, if you believe that it is inappropriate to do one action or another in your campaign, the states have the constitutional right to regulate it.

QUESTIONNER #7: My question has to do with cruel and unusual punishments. I direct it to anyone who cares to answer it. The American president has called for waterboarding anyone suspected of terrorism. Isn't that unconstitutional under the Eighth Amendment?

MADISON: One must inquire, upon whom is the President ordering such punishment? The Constitution, by its very nature, embraces citizens of the United States, and the Bill of Rights guarantees them against cruel and unusual punishments. But if the President orders such punishment upon those who are not citizens of the United States and therefore not subject to the protections of the Constitution, my political inclination would be to avoid arousing the public fervor by not ordering such punishment.

HAMILTON: I would offer this as the creator of what you now call your Coast Guard, the Revenue Service in my day. I reminded the captains of the ships that they were to treat those they ran across, be they privateers or citizens, with respect and dignity. I would hope that message is not lost in your day.

QUESTIONNER #8: Under our criminal justice system, there is a presumption of innocence for someone accused of a crime until that person is convicted. It doesn't work that way in many other countries. How did that come to be here?

HENRY: As the most successful attorney upon the dais, I shall attempt to answer your question . The idea that one is presumed innocent until proven guilty is an ancient philosophy that goes all the way back to the Bible itself, to Genesis. Though we Americans separated ourselves from the government and crown in Great Britain, and despite shortcomings of the previous five or six generations, we were always proud to be British, the people most blessed with liberty and the best form of government in the world. And we continue to embrace those traditions. True, we threw out the old—a constitutional monarchy—and replaced it with the new—a republican system of government. But we continue to embrace the principles we hold in common. Presumption of innocence is one of them. One of the greatest legal minds of the 18h century was William Blackstone. He had a maxim: It is better that ten guilty people escape than that one innocent person should suffer.

MODERATOR: I would like to close off this part of our program with a question for Mr. Jefferson. Sir, some have questioned whether the President might be in violation of the First Amendment guarantee of freedom of the press. We keep hearing accusations of fake news. He has even threatened to shut down some news organizations that are critical of him. How do you view the role of the press in our democracy?

JEFFERSON: I emphasized earlier how worthy our First Amendment is, recognizing those inherent rights that are given to the family of man, not by any government, not by any ruler, those rights that are given to man by nature and nature's god, the first and foremost amongst them to hold an opinion freely and to freely express one's opinion, and that of course allows for the freedom of the press. That is not to say that all newspapers print the facts. No, I would agree, they do not, because certain newspapers become known as tabloids. They are the ones you cannot depend upon. They are the ones that print twistifications of the facts, deceits and lies. Yet you are free to peruse them as you choose. So I would be concerned about preferring a tabloid over a newspaper that you can depend upon. And therefore, as I have written and pronounce once more, were it left to me to decide whether we should have this nation with a government and no newspapers or have this nation with newspapers and no government, I would not hesitate for a moment but to accept the latter. Who must be informed? Who must make up their minds as to what they read in the newspapers? What American citizens would seek to satisfy themselves by reading only one newspaper for what they want to read without reading the opposite opinion and then making up their mind for what is best for everyone. It is an ancient adage, citizens, wherever the press is free, the people will be free.

MODERATOR: Thank you, gentlemen, for your wisdom and insights. *(He turns to Patrick Henry.)* Mr. Henry, I want to come back to you for the last part of the program. In Episode 1 we discussed Mr. Jefferson's Declaration of Independence and how it all started with his election to the Second Continental Congress.

HENRY: I remember it well. The Virginia Convention in Richmond.

MODERATOR: It was also at that convention that you gave the most famous speech of your life, the one that inspired your fellow Virginians and eventually all the other colonies to take up arms against the British.

HENRY: Indeed.

MODERATOR: Can you tell us what led to that speech?

HENRY: After George III rejected our latest petition of grievances, I moved that Virginia be put into a state of defense. Cries of protest filled the room. That's when I rose to speak.

MODERATOR: Can you set the scene for us?

HENRY: It was the 23rd of March, 1775, at St. John's Church in Richmond. *(He rises to speak.)* "The question before this house is one of awful moment to this country. For my own part, it is considered nothing less than a question of freedom or slavery. Should I keep back my opinions at such a time through fear of giving offense, I should consider myself guilty of treason.

"It is natural for men to indulge in the illusions of hope. We are apt to shut our eyes against a painful truth—and listen to the song of that siren until she transforms us into beasts. Is this the part of wise men, engaged in a great and arduous struggle for liberty?

"I have but one lamp by which my feet our guided, and that is the lamp of experience. I know no way of judging the future but by the past. And judging by the past, I wish to know, what has there been in the conduct of the British ministry to justify (our hopes)? Is it that insidious smile with which our petition has lately been received?

"Trust it not, my friends. It will prove a snare to your feet. Suffer not yourselves to be betrayed with a kiss. Ask yourselves how this gracious reception of our petition comports with those warlike preparations which cover our waters and darken our land. Are fleets and armies necessary to a work of conciliation? Have we shown ourselves so unwilling to be reconciled that force must be called in to win back our love? Let us not deceive ourselves. These are the implements of war and subjugation—the last arguments to which kings resort.

"Our petitions have been slighted...our supplications have been disregarded, and we have been spurned with contempt from the foot of the throne. In vain, after all these things, may we indulge the fond hope of peace and reconciliation. If we wish to be free...we must fight! I repeat it, we must fight! An appeal to arms and to the God of hosts is all that is left us!"

"They tell us that we are weak. But when shall we be stronger? The battle is not to the strong alone; it is to the vigilant, the active,

"Our chains are forged. Their clanking may be heard on the plains of Boston! The war is inevitable. Let it come! I repeat it, let it come! Gentlemen may cry peace, peace—but there is no peace. The next gale that sweeps from the north will bring to our ears the clash of resounding arms! Our brethren are already in the field! Why stand we here idle? What is it that we wish? Is life so dear, or peace so sweet, as to be purchased at the price of chains or slavery? Forbid it, Almighty God!

"I know not what course others may take, but as for me, give me liberty—or give me death!"

MODERATOR: And so, ladies and gentlemen, we end this series on the same note where it began: our love of liberty. Whatever differences we may have as Americans—no matter where we fall in the political spectrum, no matter what grievances we have with one another—let us remember that one thing we have in common. As our Founders put it, *E pluribus unum:* Out of many, we are one. Our union may be imperfect, but what unites us is our love of liberty. For more than two hundred years, it's what our country has stood for. For more than two hundred years, it has been our beacon of light to the world. May it never go out.

Now, on behalf of James Madison, Thomas Jefferson, Alexander Hamilton and Patrick Henry, thank you and God bless.

SOURCE NOTES

I'm appending these source notes for two reasons: first, to suggest additional reading if you're inspired to learn more about what our Founding Fathers said and did to bring this country into being; second, to prove I'm not making this stuff up. —MJN

EPISODE 1: MAKING A NATION

6 *"It started with molasses":* While Lexington is considered the flashpoint of the American Revolution, in reality there were several other, less dramatic, events that led up to it. John Adams cites the Navigation Act of 1733 (a.k.a. the Molasses Act) as the first of those events. For more on the role played by the Navigation Acts see Lewis Paul Todd, *Rise of the American Nation* (New York: Harcourt Brace, 1966), 56-59.

6 *"Then and there the child Independence was born":* John Adams, *Novanglus; and Massachusettensis*, quoted in Catherine Drinker Bowen, *John Adams and the American Revolution* (New York: Crosset & Dunlap, 1976), 217. Also see Richard B. Morris, "Then and there the child Independence was born," *American Heritage* (February 1962), 36.

7 *"...the Boston riot":* The Boston Massacre didn't become known by that name until years later. Paul Revere's engraving (see p. 9) refers

to "The Bloody Massacre perpetrated in King Street." In the early 1800s it was called the State Street Massacre. Adams himself used the term "riot" in his speech to the jury in defense of the redcoats: www.bostonmassacre.net/trial/acct-adams1.htm.

8 *"...the first world war":* In Europe the Seven Years War was fought between an alliance of France, Russia, Sweden, Austria and Saxony against Prussia, Hanover and Great Britain. The war took on international significance as Britain and France fought for domination of North America and India, hence the term "*first* world war." Robert Wilde, "The Seven Years War 1756-63," About.com Guide.

8 *"...a motley rabble of saucy boys":* Adams's speech in defense of the redcoats, quoted in David McCullough, *John Adams* (New York: Simon & Schuster, 2001), 67. Also see www.bostonmassacre.net/trial/acct-adams1.htm.

8 *"I devoted myself to endless labor and anxiety": The Works of John Adams, Vol. 2,* Charles Francis Adams, ed. (Cambridge University Press, 2011), 232.

9 *"My cousin, Sam Adams":* John Adams was in fact a second cousin of Samuel Adams, the radical Boston patriot. For more on their relationship see David McCullough, *John Adams*, 20.

9 *"Sam was a maltster":* Pauline Maier, "Samuel Adams," *American National Biography* (New York: Oxford University Press, 1979). For more on Samuel Adams's failed business ventures see Mark Puls, *Samuel Adams: Father of the American Revolution* (New York: Palgrave Macmillan, 2006), 28.

9 *"...the Boston Tea Party":* Like the Boston Massacre, the Boston Tea Party didn't become known by that name until later. David McCullough, *John Adams,* 70.

10 *"A stitch in time saves nine":* This aphorism and the three that follow appeared originally in *Poor Richard's Almanack*, published between 1732 and 1758. For more on *Poor Richard's Almanack,* see Walter Isaacson, *Benjamin Franklin: An American Life* (New York: Simon & Schuster, 2003), 94.

11 *"Time delays were the hobgoblin of diplomacy":* a variation of Ralph Waldo Emerson's famous quotation, "A foolish consistency is the hobgoblin of little minds." Liberty taken by the author.

12 *"Not a Word of her Face":* Benjamin Franklin's song to his wife, Deborah (c. 1742). *Benjamin Franklin: A Biography in His Own Words,* Thomas Fleming, ed. (New York: Harper & Row, 1972), 70.

13 *"... the stamp tax":* The attack on Franklin's house in Philadelphia and his subsequent opposition to the stamp tax are described in detail in Gordon S. Wood, *The Americanization of Benjamin Franklin* (New York: Penguin Books, 2004), 105-113. Also see Walter Isaacson, *Benjamin Franklin: An American Life,* 223.

13 *"e pluribus unum":* a Latin phrase meaning "out of many, one." Franklin proposed this phrase for the Great Seal of the United States in 1776. Congress adopted it as the national motto in 1782. *Columbia Electronic Encyclopedia* (Columbia University Press, 2013): www.cc.columbia.edu/cu/cup/.

14 *"He brought with him a reputation for literature":* John Adams letter to Timothy Pickering (August 6, 1822). *The Works of John Adams,*

Vol. 2, Charles Francis Adams, ed. (Cambridge University Press, 2011), 113

14 *"I made an agreement with John":* Jefferson made his violin agreement with John Randolph in 1771. For the text see *The Papers of Thomas Jefferson, Vol. 1,* Julian P. Boyd, ed. (Princeton University Press, 1969), 66.

15 *"I wrote him the longest letter":* Franklin's letter to his son William is lost but is described in *Benjamin Franklin: A Biography in His Own Words,* Thomas Fleming, ed. (New York: Harper & Row, 1972), 263.

15 *"Nothing ever hurt me so much":* Benjamin Franklin to his son William (August 16, 1784); letter quoted in Walter Isaacson, *Benjamin Franklin: An American Life,* 430.

16 *"He was the laziest man for reading I ever knew": The Autobiography of Thomas Jefferson* (New York: Empire Books, 2012), 15. Jefferson's criticisms of Patrick Henry's oratory "betrayed a certain admiration for Henry's capacity to sway a crowd by emotional appeals unencumbered with any learning or evidence": Joseph L. Ellis, *American Sphinx: The Character of Thomas Jefferson* (New York: Vintage Books, 1998), 44.

18 *"'Scarcely have our minds been able to emerge'":* Thomas Jefferson, *A Summary View of the Rights of British America* (1774); text printed in full in *The Papers of Thomas Jefferson, Vol. 1,* Julian P. Boyd, ed. (Princeton University Press, 1969), 121-135.

18 *"'A free people claim their rights'":* Ibid., 134.

19 *"Tamer sentiments were preferred":* Henry Stephens Randall, *The Life of Thomas Jefferson, Vol. 1* (Classic Reprint, 2012), *98.*

19 *"We must all hang together, or most assuredly we will all hang separately":* Franklin reportedly said this in reply to John Hancock who remarked at the signing of the Declaration of Independence, "We must be unanimous; there must be no pulling different ways." See www.wideworldofquotes.com.

20 *"Hancock listened with visible pleasure":* From John Adams's *Autobiography,* 1802-7; quoted in *John Adams, A Biography in His Own Words,* James Bishop Peabody, ed. (New York: Newsweek, 1973), 170.

20 *"It embarrassed every exertion we made in Congress":* Joseph Cowley, *John Adams: Architect of Freedom* (iUniverse, 2009*), 47.*

20 *"...a piddling genius":* John Adams letter to James Warren (July 24, 1775). *Adams Papers,* Massachusetts Historical Society; quoted in David McCullough, *John Adams,* 95.

21 *"...Letters from a Farmer in Pennsylvania":* John Dickinson published 12 letters under the name "A Farmer" in 1767 and 1768; available online at www.earlyamerica.com.

21 *"...Declaration of the Causes of Taking Up Arms":* Text printed in full in *The Papers of Thomas Jefferson, Vol. 1,* Julian P. Boyd, ed. (Princeton University Press, 1969), 187-192.

22 *"...Olive Branch Petition":* www.revolutionary-war-and-beyond.com.

22 *"...deceit and hostility and fire and sword:"* John Adams letter to James Warren (July 6, 1775). Massachusetts Historical Society; www.masshist.org/publications.

22 *"Johnny...you will be hanged":* Dickinson quoted in *John Adams: A Biography in His Own Words,* James Bishop Peabody, ed. (New York: Newsweek, 1973), 173.

22 *"I believe I would have shot myself":* Adams quoted in David McCullough, *John Adams,* 94. In his *Autobiography,* Adams wrote that Dickinson's mother and wife "would make me the most miserable man alive." Ibid., 173.

23 *"Natural law":* The discussion of natural law generally reflects the speakers' views. For a more detailed discussion, see Carl Becker, *The Declaration of Independence: A Study in the History of Political Ideas* (New York: Vintage Books, 1942), 24-79.

25 *"...I never heard him utter three sentences together":* John Adams, *Autobiography;* quoted in *John Adams: A Biography in His Own Words,* James Bishop Peabody, ed. (New York: Newsweek, 1973), 200.

25 *"The committee...appointed Mr. Jefferson and me to make the draft":* John Adams letter to Timothy Pickering (August 6, 1822). *The Works of John Adams, Vol. 2,* Charles Francis Adams, ed. (Cambridge University Press, 2011), 113.

26 *"(Thomas Paine's Common Sense) did more to turn the tide": John Adams: A Biography in His Own Words,* James Bishop Peabody, ed. (New York: Newsweek, 1973), 180.

27 *"For the next two weeks":* R.B. Bernstein, *Thomas Jefferson* (Oxford University Press, 2005), 32.

28 *"'We hold these truths to be self-evident'":* Most historians believe that Franklin suggested "self-evident" to replace "sacred and undeniable" in Jefferson's draft. A strong case can be made that he borrowed the term from Euclid's *Elements,* which was widely taught in colonial classrooms. See transcript of 2008 interview with Keith Devlin, professor of mathematics, Stanford University: npr.org/templates/story/story.php?storyId=18045610.

29 *"I tremble that God's justice cannot sleep forever":* Inscribed at the Jefferson Memorial, the complete quotation reads as follows: "Indeed, I tremble for my country that God is just, and that his justice cannot sleep forever." Thomas Jefferson, *Notes on the State of Virginia, Query XVIII.* Reprinted in *The Life and Selected Writings of Thomas Jefferson,* Adrienne Koch and William Peden, eds. (New York: Random House, 1944), 279.

29 *"I admire the high tone and flights of oratory":* John Adams letter to Timothy Pickering (August 6, 1822). *The Works of John Adams,* Vol. 2, Charles Francis Adams, ed. (Cambridge University Press, 2001), 113.

29 *"...an expression of the American mind":* Thomas Jefferson letter to Henry Lee (May 8, 1825). *Thomas Jefferson: Writings,* Merrill D. Peterson, ed. (New York: Library of America, 1984), 1500.

30 *"...the 2nd day of July":* John Adams letter to Abigail Adams (July 3, 1776). *John Adams: A Biography in His Own Words,* James Bishop Peabody, ed. (New York: Newsweek, 1973), 208.

30 *"I argued myself hoarse":* Or as Jefferson put it, fought "fearlessly for every word." "He (Adams) was the pillar of its support on the floor of Congress." David McCullough, *John Adams,* 135.

31 *"'John Thompson, Hatter'"*: Ibid., 131.

31 *"They mangled it"*: As the result of Congress's editing, Jefferson "maintained a wounded sense of betrayal by the Congress throughout the remainder of his life": Joseph L. Ellis, *American Sphinx: The Character of Thomas Jefferson* (New York: Vintage Books, 1998), 71.

EPISODE 2: MAKING A GOVERNMENT

38 *"I always talk better when I'm lying"*: a variation of James Madison's famous last words, "I always talk better lying down." The quotation appears in such popular reference books as Joseph Nathan Kane's *Facts about the Presidents* and *The World Almanac of Presidential Facts* and can be found on the Web under "Madison's last words." Also see Irving Brandt, *James Madison: Commander-in-Chief* (New York: Bobbs-Merrill, 1961), 520.

38 *"...you'd get your ears nailed to a pillory"*: The punishment for perjury was especially severe for non-whites. In May 1723 the Virginia House of Burgesses decreed that any "Negro, Mulatto, or Indian found to have given false testimony shall have one ear nailed to the pillory, and there stand for the space of one hour, and then the said ear to be cut off; and thereafter the other ear nailed in like manner, and cut off...and moreover to (have) thirty-nine lashes well laid on his or her bare back." *Statutes of Virginia* (1723), Vol. 127, accessible on the Web under "Perjury Penalties in Colonial Virginia." Also see "Colonial Crimes and Punishments," Colonial Williamsburg Official History Site.

38 *"Have you seen his library at Monticello?"*: Jefferson's personal library, believed to be the largest in the country, included leather-

bound copies of all the laws passed in Colonial Virginia since the founding of Jamestown. After the British burned the U.S. Capitol in the War of 1812, Congress purchased Jefferson's library—some 6,500 volumes—for $23,950 and used them to replenish the Capitol library, which became the Library of Congress. See www.loc.gov/exhibits/jefferson/jefflib.html.

38 *"I was but twenty-five years old when I came under his influence":* Irving Brandt describes Madison's early association with Jefferson in *James Madison: The Virginia Revolutionist* (New York: Bobbs-Merrill, 1941), 272-282.

39 *"I was frail, slight of build, of nervous temperament":* Garry Wills, *James Madison* (New York: Henry Holt and Co., 2002), 3. For a litany of Madison's physical maladies see Irving Brandt, *James Madison: The Virginia Revolutionist,* 98-100.

39 *"The punishment for slander was to have a spike driven through your tongue":* See "Colonial Crimes and Punishments," Colonial WilliamsburgOfficial History Site.

39 *"I got our governor, Edmund Randolph, to introduce it":* Garry Wills, *James Madison,* 25.

40 *"The term itself—'republican' with a small 'r'—was pejorative":* Gordon Wood notes that the term *republican* was "something to hang on the head of an opponent in order to damage his credibility, if not his loyalty to the crown." See Gordon Wood, *The Idea of America: Reflections on the Birth of the United States* (New York: Penguin Press, 2011), 61.

40 *"...In the 18th century monarchy was the rule":* Calling the 18th Century "the age of the republican revolution," Wood describes how monarchies that existed for centuries were overthrown and replaced by republican governments. Ibid., 57.

40 *"Monarchy had history on its side:"* Ibid., 57

41 *"My birth was the subject of the most humiliating criticism":* Alexander Hamilton letter to William Jackson, August 26, 1800. Quoted in Ron Chernow, *Alexander Hamilton* (New York: Penguin Books, 2004), 8, 615.

41 *"The bastard brat of a Scottish peddler":* John Adams letter to Benjamin Rush (January 25, 1806). Quoted in Chernow, 522. Adams's opinion of Hamilton obviously never changed, even after the latter's death.

42 *"Then she contracted a fever and died":* Rachel Faucett's death left young Alexander and his brother reduced to orphans after their father's desertion. Ibid., 24

42 *"My brother and I were adopted by a cousin who committed suicide":* Ibid., \26.

42 *"My real name could be Alexander Stevens":* Ibid., 27-28.

43 *"I sailed to Boston and never looked back':* Or as Chernow puts it, "He took his unhappy boyhood, tucked it away in a mental closet, and never opened the door again." Ibid., 39.

43 *"It wasn't until Yorktown that I learned firsthand how powerless Congress was:"* Catherine Drinker Bowen observes: "The

Confederation, resting only on good faith, had no power to collect taxes, defend the country, pay the public debt, let alone encourage trade and commerce." See Bowen's *Miracle at Philadelphia: The Story of the Constitutional Convention* (New York: Back Bay Books, republished 1986), 5

43 *"Each member chipped in a dollar from his own pocket"*: Ibid., 5

44 *"New Jersey...was like a cask tapped at both ends":* Ibid., 9.

44 *"Most of our political evils stem from commercial ones"*: James Madison letter to Thomas Jefferson (March 18, 1786). Ibid., 10.

45 *"'The United States exhibit melancholy proof'":* George Washington letter to Henry Lee (October 31, 1786). Quoted in Richard Beeman, *Plain, Honest Men: The Making of the American Constitution* (New York: Random House, 2009), 17. For staging purposes Hamilton has the letter in his possession.

46 *"A gift from Marie-Antoinette:"* Beeman describes Franklin's arrival at the convention in his sedan chair. Ibid., 79-80. See also Chernow, *Alexander Hamilton,* 230.

47 *"'Succeeded' was the word he used":* When Jefferson reported for duty, the French foreign minister asked, "Is it you who replaces Dr. Franklin?" To which Jefferson famously replied, "No one can replace him, Sir. I am only his successor." Dumas Malone adds that Jefferson's "proper reply to questioners was that he did not replace Franklin. He could not do that and nobody could. He merely succeeded him." Dumas Malone, *Jefferson and the Rights of Man* (Boston: Little, Brown and Co., 1951), 33.

49 *"I...got run over by a carriage":* While claiming the loss of Gouverneur Morris's leg was "a tax on my heart," John Jay, disdainful of Morris's philandering habits, said he was "tempted to wish he had lost *something* else." Richard Beeman, *Plain, Honest Men*, 48.

49 *"'An assembly of demigods'":* Thomas Jefferson letter to John Adams (August 30, 1787). Julian Boyd et al., *The Papers of Thomas Jefferson,* 17 vols. (Princeton, N.J.: Princeton University Press, 1950—), vol. 12, 69. Notes Richard Beeman: Jefferson was "the least likely to ascribe the work of the framers of the Constitution to divine intervention." Richard Beeman, *Plain, Honest Men,* 450.

49 *"If men were angels, no government would be necessary":* James Madison, *The Federalist, No. 51.* See *The Federalist Papers,* Clinton Rossiter, ed. (New York: Penguin Group, 2003), 319.

50 *"I wrote Mr. Jefferson in Paris":* Catherine Drinker Bowen describes Jefferson's response to Madison's request for books. In return, "Madison sent Jefferson grafts of American trees for Jefferson to show in France, pecan nuts, pippin apples, cranberries, though he failed in shipping the opossums Jefferson asked for." Bowen, *Miracle in Philadelphia*, 14.

50 *"I had the pleasure of making Voltaire's acquaintance":* Walter Isaacson describes Franklin and Voltaire meeting twice in 1778. See Isaacson, *Benjamin Franklin: An American Life* (New York: Simon & Schuster, 2003), 354-355.

51 *"We served the public without pay:"* Ron Chernow writes: "(Franklin) had opposed salaries for executive-branch officers, hoping such a measure would produce civic-minded leaders, not government officials feeding at the public trough." See Chernow, *Alexander Hamilton,* 230.

51 *"...under a mulberry tree in my courtyard":* Richard Beeman, *Plain, Honest Men,* 35.

52 *"...on May 25th, we had enough delegates":* James Madison, *The Debates in the Federal Convention of 1797.* www.constitution.org/dfc/dfc_0525.htm.

52 *"...had the deliberations been open": Papers of Alexander Hamilton,* vol. 12, 355; quoted in Ron Chernow, *Alexander Hamilton* (New York: Penguin Books, 2004), 228.

52 *"Charles Pinckney...accused us":* James Madison, *The Debates in the Federal Convention of 1797.* www.constitution.org/dfc/dfc_0530.htm.

53 *"What was being proposed was a federal government, not a national one":* Ibid.

53 *"...a complete and compulsive operation":* Ibid.

54 *"You know what (the word senate) means, don't you?"* Merriam-Webster's Online Dictionary: *senate.* Origin: Latin *senatus,* from *sen-, senex* old, old man.

54 *"...wise and sober consideration":* Observes Richard Beeman: "In Madison's view... states frequently enacted 'vicious legislation,' too often prompted by the whims of public opinion rather than sober reflection." Beeman's *Plain, Honest Men,* 28.

54 *"A democracy doesn't admit vigorous execution":* from Alexander Hamilton's speech to the Federal Convention on June 18, 1787; quoted in Gerald Stourzh, *Alexander Hamilton and the Idea of*

Republic Government (Stanford University Press, 1970), 39. Also see Madison's account of Hamilton's speech: www.constitution.org/dfc/dfc_0618.

55 *"Alas, the fate of America was suspended by a hair":* Richard Brookhiser, *Gentleman Revolutionary: Gouverneur Morris, The Rake Who Wrote the Constitution* (New York: Free Press, 2003), 81.

55 *"The last thing we needed was foreign aid":* Ron Chernow, *Alexander Hamilton,* 235.

56 *"I observed how ecclesiastical benefices:"* Dr. Franklin quoted in Madison's notes of the Convention: www.constitution.org/dfc/dfc_0612.htm.

57 *"My situation is disagreeable":* Hamilton's speech advocating a monarchy is quoted in part by Ron Chernow in *Alexander Hamilton,* 231-235. Madison's notes can be found at www.constitution.org/dfc/dfc_0618.htm. The website provides links to other delegates' notes as well.

57 *"What our government needs is a principle capable of resisting the popular current":* Ibid.

57 *"...I shall take my leave":* On June 29, after the convention rejected his call for a monarchy, Hamilton "packed up and returned to New York." Ron Chernow, *Alexander Hamilton,* 235.

58 *"My dear general...how happy I am to see you look so well":* Ibid., 240.

59 *"I despair myself of seeing a favorable issue to the convention":* Ibid., 236.

59 *"...the small states fear their liberties will be in danger":* Franklin quoted by Milton Nieuwsma, Keynote Address, Riverside Centennial Celebration of the U.S. Constitution, Riverside, Illinois (September 30, 1987).

59 *"When a cabinet maker makes a table":* Ibid.

59 *"We are sent hither to consult, not to contend":* Dr. Franklin quoted in Madison's notes of the Convention: www.constitution.org/dfc/dfc_0611.

62 *"I confess...that I do not approve":* On the convention's last day, Madison recorded in his journal: "Doct. Franklin rose with a speech in his hand, which he had reduced to writing for his own conveniency, and which Mr. Wilson read." www.constitution.org/dfc/dfc_0917.htm.

62 *"No man's ideas are more remote":* Hamilton quoted in Madison's journal. Ibid.

63 *"I have the happiness to know that it's a rising sun":* According to Madison, Franklin made this remark "while the last members were signing (the instrument)." Ibid.

63 *"...a republic—if we can keep it":* According to James McHenry, a delegate from Maryland, a woman accosted Franklin as he was leaving the Pennsylvania State House and asked him, "Well, doctor, what have we got, a republic or a monarcy?" To which he replied, "A republic, madam, if you can keep it." Walter Isaacson, *Benjamin Franklin,* 459.

EPISODE 3: LIBERTY FOR ALL

71 *"Sir, the reason I objected"*: Edmund Randolph, governor of Virginia, offered to appoint Patrick Henry to the Constitutional Convention, but Henry declined on the grounds he could not afford the expense. Thad Tate, *Patrick Henry: American National Biography Online.* Accessed August 2, 2017.

71 *"I was born on a plantation in Virginia"*: Henry married his first wife, Sarah Shelton, in 1754. As a wedding gift her father gave the couple six slaves and a 300-acre farm. Henry Mayer, *A Son of Thunder: Patrick Henry and the American Republic* (New York: Grove Press, 1986), 45-48.

72 *"After that my wife had a mental breakdown:"* Sarah died in 1775 leaving Henry with six children. She may have suffered from postpartum psychosis, which then had no cure. John Kukla, *Patrick Henry: Champion of Liberty* (New York: Simon & Schuster, 2017), 158-160.

72 *"More came after I married my second wife:"* Henry married Dorothea Spotswood Dandridge on October 9, 1777, three months after being re-elected governor of Virginia. Thomas S. Kidd, *Patrick Henry: First Among Patriots* (New York: Basic Books, 2011), 138.

72 *"I remember eavesdropping at the door"*: Dumas Malone, *Jefferson the Virginian* (Boston: Little, Brown, 1948), 92.

73 *"He was the laziest man for reading I ever knew"*: Ibid., 90-91.

73 *"I said I smelt a rat":* Thomas S. Kidd, *Patrick Henry: First Among Patriots,* 182-183.

74 *"It is the best commentary on the principles government": Thomas Jefferson: Establishing a Federal Republic,* Library of Congress website, www.loc.gov/exhibits/jefferson/jefffed.html

74 *"In Federalist No. 1":* All 85 essays by Alexander Hamilton, James Madison and John Jay, along with an introduction and notes by Charles R. Kesler and copies of the Constitution, Declaration of Independence and the Articles of Confederation, are contained in *The Federalist Papers* edited by Clinton Rossiter (New York: Penguin Group, 1999).

76 *"In Massachusetts, at their ratifying convention": Introduction to the Massachusetts Ratifying Convention,* Teaching American History, www.teachingamericanhistory.org/resources/ratification/massachusetts/.

76 *"Mr. Henry rose in opposition":* After the Philadelphia Convention, Henry, along with Samuel Adams and Richard Henry Lee, publicly opposed the Constitution. They became known as the Anti-Federalists. They feared that individual rights would be quashed under a strong national government and that the president would become a king. *The Founders' Constitution* (University of Chicago Press), 195.

76 *"Gentlemen, whither is the spirit of America gone":* Pauline Maier, *Ratification: The People Debate the Constitution, 1787-1788* (New York: Simon & Schuster, 2010), 260-261.

77 *"89 in favor, 79 against":* Ibid., 308.

78 *"New Hampshire was the ninth state to ratify":* Ibid., 430.

90 *"Give me liberty—or give me death!":* Henry's famous speech, delivered extemporaneously, was pieced together by his first biographer, William Wirt, from recollections of Thomas Jefferson and others at the 1775 Virginia Convention. The full speech may be accessed at www.history.org/almanack/life/politics/giveme.cfm.

RECOMMENDED READING

For readers who desire to learn more about our Founding Fathers and the history they shaped the following books are recommended:

Beeman, Richard R. *Plain, Honest Men: The Making of the Constitution*. New York: Random House (2009).

Beeman, Richard. *Our Lives, Our Fortunes & Our Sacred Honor: The Forging of American Independence.* New York: Basic Books (2013).

Bowen, Catherine Drinker. *Miracle at Philadelphia: The Story of the Constitutional Convention.* Boston: Little, Brown (1966).

Brookhiser, Richard. *James Madison.* New York: Basic Books (2013).

Chernow, Ron. *Alexander Hamilton.* New York: Penguin Books (2005).

Chernow, Ron. *Washington: A Life.* New York: Penguin Books (2011).

Ellis, Joseph J. *Founding Brothers: The Revolutionary Generation.* New York:Vintage Books (2002).

Isaacson, Walter. *Benjamin Franklin: An American Life.* New York: Simon &Schuster (2003).

McCullough, David. *John Adams.* New York: Simon & Schuster (2001).

Meacham, Jon. *Thomas Jefferson: President & Philosopher.* Crown Books for Young Readers (2014).

Padover, Saul K. *Jefferson: A Great American's Life and Ideas.* New AmericanLibrary (1970, abridged version).

Wood, Gordon S. *The Idea of America: Reflections on the Birth of the United States.* New York: Penguin Press (2011).

DISCUSSION/STUDY QUESTIONS

Comprehensive, age-appropriate teaching resources, along with videos of all three episodes, may be downloaded from www.inventing-america.org.

The following questions are drawn from those resources:

EPISODE 1: MAKING A NATION

1. According to John Adams, when did the American Revolution begin?
2. Why was Parliament taxing the American colonies?
3. Why did John Adams defend the British soldiers charged with murder after the Boston Massacre? What was the verdict?
4. According to John Adams, what was "the last straw" for the colonists? What was his response?
5. Why was Benjamin Franklin frustrated with Pennsylvania's government?
6. What was the Stamp Act?
7. How did Thomas Jefferson argue that the American colonists did not have to follow the laws of Parliament?
8. Read the passage from *A Summary View of the Rights of British America* that Thomas Jefferson quotes on pp. 17-18. What is he saying in this passage? How was it received by the delegates? By Parliament?

9. Describe the delegates' relationships with each other and their fellow patriots.
10. Why did John Adams nominate George Washington over John Hancock to command the Continental Army?
11. What did John Dickinson say in his *Declaration of the Causes of Taking Up Arms*? How did it differ from what he wrote in the *Olive Branch Petition*?
12. Why did Mr. Dickinson change his mind about the revolution and oppose the war?
13. What did Thomas Jefferson mean by "natural law"? How is this different from common law?
14. What document helped turn the tide in favor of independence?
15. What were the main arguments between the radicals and conservatives over declaring independence?
16. Why was natural law a more convincing argument than common law in justifying independence from Great Britain?
17. A five-man committee was appointed to write the Declaration of Independence. Two were put on the committee for geographical reasons" Why did the Continental Congress select committee members based on the colonies they represented and not on their writing abilities?
18. What are the major ideas expressed in the Declaration of Independence and their intellectual origins?
19. The following statement was in the original draft of the Declaration: "The Christian king of Great Britain has waged cruel war against human nature in the persons of a distant people who never offended him, captivating and carrying them into slavery in another hemisphere." Why was it taken out?
20. What role, if any, did religion play in the independence movement?

EPISODE 2: MAKING A GOVERNMENT

1. Why did the Founding Fathers call the Constitutional Convention?
2. What did Thomas Jefferson mean when he called the Convention "an assembly of demigods"? Do you agree?
3. What were some of the issues with the Articles and Confederation?
4. Why was the Virginia Plan so radical in a world of 18th century monarchies?
5. What friendships and rivalries played into the constitutional debates?
6. What were the different plans considered by the delegates, and why were they rejected?
7. What models did our Founding Fathers use in constructing the federal government?
8. The Constitutional Convention split into two groups. What were they called? What did they want?
9. Where did the word "senate" come from?
10. What is the difference between a democracy and a republic?
11. What compromises were required to secure approval of the Constitution?
12. Do you see compromise happening in politics today? In what ways? Why or why not?
13. How did Gouverneur Morris explain the difference between a federal government and a national government. Are they any different?
14. What are the fundamental ideas behind the distribution of powers and checks and balances established by the Constitution?
15. Why did Benjamin Franklin believe the chief executive should not be paid?
16. How was the issue of slavery resolved at the Convention?
17. What was the Great Compromise?
18. Why is the phrase "We the people" so important?

19. George Washington predicted the new federal government wouldn't last twenty years. What would he say if could come back?
20. What features of the Constitution have made it the most enduring and widely imitated in world history?

EPISODE 3: LIBERTY FOR ALL

1. What were the main influences on the United States Bill of Rights?
2. What event pushed Thomas Jefferson to argue for a Bill of Rights to be added to the Constitution?
3. What were the main arguments for adding a Bill of Rights to the Constitution?
4. What were the arguments against adding a Bill of Rights?
5. What was the Federalist movement?
6. What was the Anti-Federalist movement?
7. What were the arguments made by the Federalists and Anti-Federalists to advance their cases in the ratification debates?
8. Why did Patrick Henry oppose the Constitution?
9. What was the single, most divisive issue with the Constitution?
10. What does the Bill of Rights tell us about what the Founding Fathers valued in 1791?
11. What individual liberties are spelled out in the Bill of Rights?
12. Do any of these liberties seem inapplicable today? Why?
13. What new amendments would you propose?
14. If Alexander Hamilton didn't like the final draft of the Constitution, why did he support it?
15. Hamilton, Madison and John Jay wrote a series of essays titled the *Federalist Papers*. What were some of the things they argued for in these essays?
16. What cases have recently come before the U.S. Supreme Court involving one or more provisions of the Bill of Rights?

17. Why do you think the Bill of Rights is the most hotly debated part of our Constitution?
18. What are some of the debates you have heard recently over the Bill of Rights?
19. How did Patrick Henry's Liberty-or-Death speech inspire the colonies to unite against the British?
20. How does his speech reflect the ideas expressed in the Bill of Rights?

The Declaration of Independence

IN CONGRESS, July 4, 1776.

The unanimous Declaration of the thirteen united States of America,

When in the Course of human events, it becomes necessary for one people to dissolve the political bands which have connected them with another, and to assume among the powers of the earth, the separate and equal station to which the Laws of Nature and of Nature's God entitle them, a decent respect to the opinions of mankind requires that they should declare the causes which impel them to the separation.

We hold these truths to be self-evident, that all men are created equal, that they are endowed by their Creator with certain unalienable Rights, that among these are Life, Liberty and the pursuit of Happiness. --That to secure these rights, Governments are instituted among Men, deriving their just powers from the consent of the governed, --That whenever any Form of Government becomes destructive of these ends, it is the Right of the People to alter or to abolish it, and to institute new Government, laying its foundation on such principles and organizing its powers in such form, as to them shall seem most likely to effect their Safety and Happiness. Prudence, indeed, will dictate that Governments long established should not be changed for light and transient causes; and accordingly all experience hath shewn, that mankind are more disposed to suffer, while evils are sufferable, than to right themselves by abolishing the forms to which they are accustomed. But when a long train of abuses and usurpations, pursuing invariably the same Object evinces a design to reduce them under absolute Despotism, it is their right, it is their duty, to throw off such Government, and to provide new Guards for their future security.–Such has been the patient sufferance of these Colonies; and such is now the necessity which constrains them to alter their former Systems of Government. The history of the present King of Great Britain is a history of repeated injuries and usurpations, all having in direct object the establishment of an absolute Tyranny over these States. To prove this, let Facts be submitted to a candid world.

He has refused his Assent to Laws, the most wholesome and necessary for the public good.

He has forbidden his Governors to pass Laws of immediate and pressing importance, unless suspended in their operation till his Assent should be obtained; and when so suspended, he has utterly neglected to attend to them.

He has refused to pass other Laws for the accommodation of large districts of people, unless those people would relinquish the right of Representation in the Legislature, a right inestimable to them and formidable to tyrants only.

He has called together legislative bodies at places unusual, uncomfortable, and distant from the depository of their public Records, for the sole purpose of fatiguing them into compliance with his measures.

He has dissolved Representative Houses repeatedly, for opposing with manly firmness his invasions on the rights of the people.

He has refused for a long time, after such dissolutions, to cause others to be elected; whereby the Legislative powers, incapable of Annihilation, have returned to the People at large for their exercise; the State remaining in the mean time exposed to all the dangers of invasion from without, and convulsions within.

He has endeavoured to prevent the population of these States; for that purpose obstructing the Laws for Naturalization of Foreigners; refusing to pass others to encourage their migrations hither, and raising the conditions of new Appropriations of Lands.

He has obstructed the Administration of Justice, by refusing his Assent to Laws for establishing Judiciary powers.

He has made Judges dependent on his Will alone, for the tenure of their offices, and the amount and payment of their salaries.

He has erected a multitude of New Offices, and sent hither swarms of Officers to harrass our people, and eat out their substance.

He has kept among us, in times of peace, Standing Armies without the Consent of our legislatures.

He has affected to render the Military independent of and superior to the Civil power.

He has combined with others to subject us to a jurisdiction foreign to our constitution, and unacknowledged by our laws; giving his Assent to their Acts of pretended Legislation:

For Quartering large bodies of armed troops among us:

For protecting them, by a mock Trial, from punishment for any Murders which they should commit on the Inhabitants of these States:

For cutting off our Trade with all parts of the world:

For imposing Taxes on us without our Consent:

For depriving us in many cases, of the benefits of Trial by Jury:

For transporting us beyond Seas to be tried for pretended offences

For abolishing the free System of English Laws in a neighbouring Province, establishing therein an Arbitrary government, and enlarging its

Boundaries so as to render it at once an example and fit instrument for introducing the same absolute rule into these Colonies:

For taking away our Charters, abolishing our most valuable Laws, and altering fundamentally the Forms of our Governments:

For suspending our own Legislatures, and declaring themselves invested with power to legislate for us in all cases whatsoever.

He has abdicated Government here, by declaring us out of his Protection and waging War against us.

He has plundered our seas, ravaged our Coasts, burnt our towns, and destroyed the lives of our people.

He is at this time transporting large Armies of foreign Mercenaries to compleat the works of death, desolation and tyranny, already begun with circumstances of Cruelty & perfidy scarcely paralleled in the most barbarous ages, and totally unworthy the Head of a civilized nation.

He has constrained our fellow Citizens taken Captive on the high Seas to bear Arms against their Country, to become the executioners of their friends and Brethren, or to fall themselves by their Hands.

He has excited domestic insurrections amongst us, and has endeavoured to bring on the inhabitants of our frontiers, the merciless Indian Savages, whose known rule of warfare, is an undistinguished destruction of all ages, sexes and conditions.

In every stage of these Oppressions We have Petitioned for Redress in the most humble terms: Our repeated Petitions have been answered only by repeated injury. A Prince whose character is thus marked by every act which may define a Tyrant, is unfit to be the ruler of a free people.

Nor have We been wanting in attentions to our Brittish brethren. We have warned them from time to time of attempts by their legislature to extend an unwarrantable jurisdiction over us. We have reminded them of the circumstances of our emigration and settlement here. We have appealed to their native justice and magnanimity, and we have conjured them by the ties of our common kindred to disavow these usurpations, which, would inevitably interrupt our connections and correspondence. They too have been deaf to the voice of justice and of consanguinity. We must, therefore, acquiesce in the necessity, which denounces our Separation, and hold them, as we hold the rest of mankind, Enemies in War, in Peace Friends.

We, therefore, the Representatives of the united States of America, in General Congress, Assembled, appealing to the Supreme Judge of the world for the rectitude of our intentions, do, in the Name, and by Authority of the good People of these Colonies, solemnly publish and declare, That these United Colonies are, and of Right ought to be Free and Independent States; that they are Absolved from all Allegiance to the British Crown, and that all political connection between them and the State of Great Britain, is and ought to be totally dissolved; and that as Free and Independent States, they have full Power to levy War, conclude Peace, contract Alliances, establish Commerce, and to do all other Acts and Things which Independent States may of right do. And for the support of this Declaration, with a firm reliance on the protection of divine Providence, we mutually pledge to each other our Lives, our Fortunes and our sacred Honor.

The 56 signatures on the Declaration:

John Hancock

Josiah Bartlett

William Whipple

Matthew Thornton

Samuel Adams

Abraham Clark

Robert Morris

Benjamin Rush

Benjamin Franklin

John Morton

John Adams
Robert Treat Paine
Elbridge Gerry
Stephen Hopkins
William Ellery
Roger Sherman
Samuel Huntington
William Williams
Oliver Wolcott
William Floyd
Philip Livingston
Francis Lewis
Lewis Morris
Richard Stockton
John Witherspoon
Francis Hopkinson
John Hart
Francis Lightfoot Lee
Carter Braxton
William Hooper
Joseph Hewes
John Penn
Edward Rutledge
George Clymer
James Smith
George Taylor
James Wilson
George Ross
George Read
Caesar Rodney
Thomas McKean
Samuel Chase
William Paca
Thomas Stone
Charles Carroll of Carrollton
George Wythe
Richard Henry Lee
Thomas Jefferson
Benjamin Harrison
Thomas Nelson, Jr.
Thomas Heyward, Jr.
Thomas Lynch, Jr.
Arthur Middleton
Button Gwinnett
Lyman Hall
George Walton

The Constitution of the United States of America

We the People of the United States, in Order to form a more perfect Union, establish justice, insure domestic Tranquility, provide for the common defense, promote the general Welfare, and secure the Blessings of Liberty to ourselves and our Posterity, do ordain and establish this Constitution for the United States of America.

ARTICLE I

Section 1. All legislative powers herein granted shall be vested in a Congress of the United States, which shall consist of a Senate and House of Representatives.

Section 2. The House of Representatives shall be composed of members chosen every second year by the people of the several states, and the electors in each state shall have the qualifications requisite for electors of the most numerous branch of the state legislature.

No person shall be a Representative who shall not have attained to the Age of twenty five Years, and been seven years a citizen of the United States, and who shall not, when elected, be an inhabitant of that state in which he shall be chosen.

[Representatives and direct taxes shall be apportioned among the several states which may be included within this union, according to their respective numbers, which shall be determined by adding to the whole number of free persons, including those bound to service for a term of years, and excluding Indians not taxed, three fifths of all other Persons.][1] The actual Enumeration shall be made within three years after the first meeting of the Congress of the United States, and within every subsequent term of ten years, in such manner as they shall by law direct. The number of Representatives shall not exceed one for every thirty thousand, but each state shall have at least one Representative; and until such enumeration shall be made, the state of New Hampshire shall be entitled to chuse three, Massachusetts eight, Rhode Island and Providence Plantations one, Connecticut five, New York six, New Jersey four, Pennsylvania eight, Delaware one, Maryland six, Virginia ten, North Carolina five, South Carolina five, and Georgia three.

When vacancies happen in the Representation from any state, the executive authority thereof shall issue writs of election to fill such vacancies.

The House of Representatives shall choose their speaker and other officers; and shall have the sole power of impeachment.

Section 3. The Senate of the United States shall be composed of two Senators from each state, [chosen by the legislature thereof,][2] for six years; and each Senator shall have one vote.

Immediately after they shall be assembled in consequence of the first election, they shall be divided as equally as may be into three classes. The seats of the Senators of the first class shall be vacated at the expiration of the second year, of the second class at the expiration of the fourth year, and the third class at the expiration of the sixth year, so that one third may be chosen every second year; [and if vacancies happen by resignation, or otherwise, during the recess of the legislature of any state, the executive thereof may make temporary appointments until the next meeting of the legislature, which shall then fill such vacancies.][3]

---

1 Changed by the Fourteenth Amendment.
2 Changed by the Seventeenth Amendment.
3 Changed by the Seventeenth Amendment.

No person shall be a Senator who shall not have attained to the age of thirty years, and been nine years a citizen of the United States and who shall not, when elected, be an inhabitant of that state for which he shall be chosen.

The Vice President of the United States shall be President of the Senate, but shall have no vote, unless they be equally divided.

The Senate shall choose their other officers, and also a President pro tempore, in the absence of the Vice President, or when he shall exercise the office of President of the United States.

The Senate shall have the sole power to try all impeachments. When sitting for that purpose, they shall be on oath or affirmation. When the President of the United States is tried, the Chief Justice shall preside: And no person shall be convicted without the concurrence of two thirds of the Members present.

Judgment in cases of impeachment shall not extend further than to removal from office, and disqualification to hold and enjoy any office of honor, trust or profit under the United States: but the party convicted shall nevertheless be liable and subject to indictment, trial, judgment and punishment, according to Law.

Section 4. The times, places and manner of holding elections for Senators and Representatives, shall be prescribed in each state by the legislature thereof; but the Congress may at any time by law make or alter such regulations, except as to the places of choosing Senators.

The Congress shall assemble at least once in every year, and such meeting shall be [on the first Monday in December,][4] unless they shall by law appoint a different day.

Section 5. Each House shall be the judge of the elections, returns and qualifications of its own members, and a majority of each shall constitute

4 Changed by the Twentieth Amendment.

a quorum to do business; but a smaller number may adjourn from day to day, and may be authorized to compel the attendance of absent members, in such manner, and under such penalties as each House may provide.

Each House may determine the rules of its proceedings, punish its members for disorderly behavior, and, with the concurrence of two thirds, expel a member.

Each House shall keep a journal of its proceedings, and from time to time publish the same, excepting such parts as may in their judgment require secrecy; and the yeas and nays of the members of either House on any question shall, at the desire of one fifth of those present, be entered on the journal.

Neither House, during the session of Congress, shall, without the consent of the other, adjourn for more than three days, nor to any other place than that in which the two Houses shall be sitting.

Section 6. The Senators and Representatives shall receive a compensation for their services, to be ascertained by law, and paid out of the treasury of the United States. They shall in all cases, except treason, felony and breach of the peace, be privileged from arrest during their attendance at the session of their respective Houses, and in going to and returning from the same; and for any speech or debate in either House, they shall not be questioned in any other place.

No Senator or Representative shall, during the time for which he was elected, be appointed to any civil office under the authority of the United States, which shall have been created, or the emoluments whereof shall have been increased during such time: and no person holding any office under the United States, shall be a member of either House during his continuance in office.

Section 7. All Bills for raising revenue shall originate in the House of Representatives; but the Senate may propose or concur with amendments as on other Bills.

Every Bill which shall have passed the House of Representatives and the Senate, shall, before it become a law, be presented to the President of the United States; if he approve he shall sign it, but if not he shall return it, with his objections to that House in which it shall have originated, who shall enter the objections at large on their journal, and proceed to reconsider it. If after such reconsideration two thirds of that House shall agree to pass the bill, it shall be sent, together with the objections, to the other House, by which it shall likewise be reconsidered, and if approved by two thirds of that House, it shall become a law. But in all such cases the votes of both Houses shall be determined by yeas and nays, and the names of the persons voting for and against the bill shall be entered on the journal of each House respectively. If any bill shall not be returned by the President within ten days (Sundays excepted) after it shall have been presented to him, the same shall be a law, in like manner as if he had signed it, unless the Congress by their adjournment prevent its return, in which case it shall not be a law.

Every order, resolution, or vote to which the concurrence of the Senate and House of Representatives may be necessary (except on a question of adjournment) shall be presented to the President of the United States; and before the same shall take effect, shall be approved by him, or being disapproved by him, shall be repassed by two thirds of the Senate and House of Representatives, according to the rules and limitations prescribed in the case of a bill.

Section 8. The Congress shall have power to lay and collect taxes, duties, imposts and excises, to pay the debts and provide for the common defense and general welfare of the United States; but all duties, imposts and excises shall be uniform throughout the United States;

To borrow money on the credit of the United States;

To regulate commerce with foreign nations, and among the several states, and with the Indian tribes;

To establish a uniform rule of naturalization, and uniform laws on the subject of bankruptcies throughout the United States;

To coin money, regulate the value thereof, and of foreign coin, and fix the standard of weights and measures;

To provide for the punishment of counterfeiting the securities and current coin of the United States;

To establish post offices and post roads;

To promote the progress of science and useful arts, by securing for limited times to authors and inventors the exclusive right to their respective writings and discoveries;

To constitute tribunals inferior to the Supreme Court;

To define and punish piracies and felonies committed on the high seas, and offenses against the law of nations;

To declare war, grant letters of marque and reprisal, and make rules concerning captures on land and water;

To raise and support armies, but no appropriation of money to that use shall be for a longer term than two years;

To provide and maintain a Navy;

To make rules for the government and regulation of the land and naval forces;

To provide for calling forth the militia to execute the laws of the union, suppress insurrections and repel invasions;

To provide for organizing, arming, and disciplining, the militia, and for governing such part of them as may be employed in the service of the United States, reserving to the states respectively, the appointment of the officers, and the authority of training the militia according to the discipline prescribed by Congress;

To exercise exclusive legislation in all cases whatsoever, over such District (not exceeding ten miles square) as may, by cession of particular states, and the acceptance of Congress, become the seat of the government of the United States, and to exercise like authority over all places purchased by the consent of the legislature of the state in which the same shall be, for the erection of forts, magazines, arsenals, dockyards, and other needful buildings;–And

To make all laws which shall be necessary and proper for carrying into execution the foregoing powers, and all other powers vested by this Constitution in the government of the United States, or in any department or officer thereof.

Section 9. The migration or importation of such persons as any of the states now existing shall think proper to admit, shall not be prohibited by the Congress prior to the year one thousand eight hundred and eight, but a tax or duty may be imposed on such importation, not exceeding ten dollars for each person.

The privilege of the writ of habeas corpus shall not be suspended, unless when in cases of rebellion or invasion the public safety may require it.

No bill of attainder or ex post facto Law shall be passed.

No capitation, or other direct, tax shall be laid, unless in proportion to the census or enumeration herein before directed to be taken.[5]

No tax or duty shall be laid on articles exported from any state.

No preference shall be given by any regulation of commerce or revenue to the ports of one state over those of another: nor shall vessels bound to, or from, one state, be obliged to enter, clear or pay duties in another.

5 Changed by the Seventeenth Amendment.

No money shall be drawn from the treasury, but in consequence of appropriations made by law; and a regular statement and account of receipts and expenditures of all public money shall be published from time to time.

No title of nobility shall be granted by the United States: and no person holding any office of profit or trust under them, shall, without the consent of the Congress, accept of any present, emolument, office, or title, of any kind whatever, from any king, prince, or foreign state.

ARTICLE II

Section 1. The executive power shall be vested in a President of the United States of America. He shall hold his office during the term of four years, and, together with the Vice President, chosen for the same term, be elected, as follows:

Each state shall appoint, in such manner as the Legislature thereof may direct, a number of electors, equal to the whole number of Senators and Representatives to which the State may be entitled in the Congress: but no Senator or Representative, or person holding an office of trust or profit under the United States, shall be appointed an elector.

[The electors shall meet in their respective states, and vote by ballot for two persons, of whom one at least shall not be an inhabitant of the same state with themselves. And they shall make a list of all the persons voted for, and of the number of votes for each; which list they shall sign and certify, and transmit sealed to the seat of the government of the United States, directed to the President of the Senate. The President of the Senate shall, in the presence of the Senate and House of Representatives, open all the certificates, and the votes shall then be counted. The person having the greatest number of votes shall be the President, if such number be a majority of the whole number of electors appointed; and if there be more than one who have such majority, and have an equal number of votes, then the House of Representatives shall immediately choose by ballot one of them for President; and if no person have a majority, then from the five highest on the list the said House shall in like manner choose the President. But in choosing the President, the votes shall be taken by States, the representation from each state having one vote; A quorum for this purpose shall consist of a member or members from two thirds of the states, and a majority of all the states shall be necessary to a choice. In every case, after the choice of the President, the person having the greatest number of votes of the electors shall be the Vice President. But if there should remain two or more who have equal votes, the Senate shall choose from them by ballot the Vice President.][6]

The Congress may determine the time of choosing the electors, and the day on which they shall give their votes; which day shall be the same throughout the United States.

No person except a natural born citizen, or a citizen of the United States, at the time of the adoption of this Constitution, shall be eligible to the office of President; neither shall any person be eligible to that office who shall not have attained to the age of thirty five years, and been fourteen Years a resident within the United States.

[In case of the removal of the President from office, or of his death, resignation, or inability to discharge the powers and duties of the said office, the same shall devolve on the Vice President, and the Congress may by law provide for the case of removal, death, resignation or inability, both of the President and Vice President, declaring what officer shall then act as President, and such officer shall act accordingly, until the disability be removed, or a President shall be elected.][7]

T

6 Changed by the Twelfth Amendment.
7 Changed by the Twenty-Fifth Amendment.

he President shall, at stated times, receive for his services, a compensation, which shall neither be increased nor diminished during the period for which he shall have been elected, and he shall not receive within that period any other emolument from the United States, or any of them.

Before he enter on the execution of his office, he shall take the following oath or affirmation:–"I do solemnly swear (or affirm) that I will faithfully execute the office of President of the United States, and will to the best of my ability, preserve, protect and defend the Constitution of the United States."

Section 2. The President shall be commander in chief of the Army and Navy of the United States, and of the militia of the several states, when called into the actual service of the United States; he may require the opinion, in writing, of the principal officer in each of the executive departments, upon any subject relating to the duties of their respective offices, and he shall have power to grant reprieves and pardons for offenses against the United States, except in cases of impeachment.

He shall have power, by and with the advice and consent of the Senate, to make treaties, provided two thirds of the Senators present concur; and he shall nominate, and by and with the advice and consent of the Senate, shall appoint ambassadors, other public ministers and consuls, judges of the Supreme Court, and all other officers of the United States, whose appointments are not herein otherwise provided for, and which shall be established by law: but the Congress may by law vest the appointment of such inferior officers, as they think proper, in the

President alone, in the courts of law, or in the heads of departments.

The President shall have power to fill up all vacancies that may happen during the recess of the Senate, by granting commissions which shall expire at the end of their next session.

Section 3. He shall from time to time give to the Congress information of the state of the union, and recommend to their consideration such measures as he shall judge necessary and expedient; he may, on extraordinary occasions, convene both Houses, or either of them, and in case of disagreement between them, with respect to the time of adjournment, he may adjourn them to such time as he shall think proper; he shall receive ambassadors and other public ministers; he shall take care that the laws be faithfully executed, and shall commission all the officers of the United States.

Section 4. The President, Vice President and all civil officers of the United States, shall be removed from office on impeachment for, and conviction of, treason, bribery, or other high crimes and misdemeanors.

ARTICLE III

Section 1. The judicial power of the United States, shall be vested in one Supreme Court, and in such inferior courts as the Congress may from time to time ordain and establish. The judges, both of the supreme and inferior courts, shall hold their offices during good behaviour, and shall, at stated times, receive for their services, a compensation, which shall not be diminished during their continuance in office.

Section 2. The judicial power shall extend to all cases, in law and equity, arising under this Constitution, the laws of the United States, and treaties made, or which shall be made, under their authority;–to all cases affecting ambassadors, other public ministers and consuls;–to all cases of admiralty and maritime jurisdiction;–to controversies to which the United States shall be a party;–to controversies between two or more states;–[between a state and citizens of another state;–][8] between citizens of different states;–

8 Changed by the Eleventh Amendment.

between citizens of the same state claiming lands under grants of different states, [and between a state, or the citizens thereof, and foreign states, citizens or subjects.][9]

In all cases affecting ambassadors, other public ministers and consuls, and those in which a state shall be party, the Supreme Court shall have original jurisdiction. In all the other cases before mentioned, the Supreme Court shall have appellate jurisdiction, both as to law and fact, with such exceptions, and under such regulations as the Congress shall make.

The trial of all crimes, except in cases of impeachment, shall be by jury; and such trial shall be held in the state where the said crimes shall have been committed; but when not committed within any state, the trial shall be at such place or places as the Congress may by law have directed.

Section 3. Treason against the United States, shall consist only in levying war against them, or in adhering to their enemies, giving them aid and comfort. No person shall be convicted of treason unless on the testimony of two witnesses to the same overt act, or on confession in open court.

The Congress shall have power to declare the punishment of treason, but no attainder of treason shall work corruption of blood, or forfeiture except during the life of the person attainted.

ARTICLE IV

Section 1. Full faith and credit shall be given in each state to the public acts, records, and judicial proceedings of every other state. And the Congress may by general laws prescribe the manner in which such acts, records, and proceedings shall be proved, and the effect thereof.

---

9 Changed by the Eleventh Amendment.

Section 2. The citizens of each state shall be entitled to all privileges and immunities of citizens in the several states.

A person charged in any state with treason, felony, or other crime, who shall flee from justice, and be found in another state, shall on demand of the executive authority of the state from which he fled, be delivered up, to be removed to the state having jurisdiction of the crime.

[No person held to service or labor in one state, under the laws thereof, escaping into another, shall, in consequence of any law or regulation therein, be discharged from such service or labor, but shall be delivered up on claim of the party to whom such service or labor may be due.][10]

Section 3. New states may be admitted by the Congress into this union; but no new states shall be formed or erected within the jurisdiction of any other state; nor any state be formed by the junction of two or more states, or parts of states, without the consent of the legislatures of the states concerned as well as of the Congress.

The Congress shall have power to dispose of and make all needful rules and regulations respecting the territory or other property belonging to the United States; and nothing in this Constitution shall be so construed as to prejudice any claims of the United States, or of any particular state.

Section 4. The United States shall guarantee to every state in this union a republican form of government, and shall protect each of them against invasion; and on application of the legislature, or of the executive (when the legislature cannot be convened) against domestic violence.

---

10 Changed by the Thirteenth Amendment.

ARTICLE V

The Congress, whenever two thirds of both houses shall deem it necessary, shall propose amendments to this Constitution, or, on the application of the legislatures of two thirds of the several states, shall call a convention for proposing amendments, which, in either case, shall be valid to all intents and purposes, as part of this Constitution, when ratified by the legislatures of three fourths of the several states, or by conventions in three fourths thereof, as the one or the other mode of ratification may be proposed by the Congress; provided that no amendment which may be made prior to the year one thousand eight hundred and eight shall in any manner affect the first and fourth clauses in the ninth section of the first article; and that no state, without its consent, shall be deprived of its equal suffrage in the Senate.

ARTICLE VI

All debts contracted and engagements entered into, before the adoption of this Constitution, shall be as valid against the United States under this Constitution, as under the Confederation.

This Constitution, and the laws of the United States which shall be made in pursuance thereof; and all treaties made, or which shall be made, under the authority of the United States, shall be the supreme law of the land; and the judges in every state shall be bound thereby, anything in the Constitution or laws of any State to the contrary notwithstanding.

The Senators and Representatives before mentioned, and the members of the several state legislatures, and all executive and judicial officers, both of the United States and of the several states, shall be bound by oath or affirmation, to support this Constitution; but no religious test shall ever be required as a qualification to any office or public trust under the United States.

ARTICLE VII

The ratification of the conventions of nine states, shall be sufficient for the establishment of this Constitution between the states so ratifying the same.

Done in convention by the unanimous consent of the states present the seventeenth day of September in the year of our Lord one thousand seven hundred and eighty seven and of the independence of the United States of America the twelfth. In witness whereof We have hereunto subscribed our Names,

G^{o}. Washington-Presidt. and deputy from Virginia

Delaware	Geo: Read Gunning Bedford jun John Dickinson Richard Bassett Jaco: Broom
Maryland	James McHenry Dan of St Thos. Jenifer Danl Carroll
Virginia	John Blair James Madison Jr.
North Carolina	Wm. Blount Richd. Dobbs Spaight Hu Williamson
South Carolina	J. Rutledge Charles Cotesworth Pinckney Charles Pinckney Pierce Butler

Georgia	William Few Abr Baldwin
New Hampshire	John Langdon Nicholas Gilman
Massachusetts	Nathaniel Gorham Rufus King
Connecticut	Wm: Saml. Johnson Roger Sherman
New York	Alexander Hamilton
New Jersey	Wil: Livingston David Brearly Wm. Paterson Jona: Dayton
Pennsylvania	B. Franklin Thomas Mifflin Robt. Morris Geo. Clymer Thos. FitzSimons Jared Ingersoll James Wilson Gouv Morris

Attest William Jackson Secretary

AMENDMENTS TO THE CONSTITUTION OF THE UNITED STATES OF AMERICA[11]

THE PREAMBLE TO THE BILL OF RIGHTS

Congress of the United States

begun and held at the City of New York, on Wednesday the fourth of March, one thousand seven hundred and eighty nine.

THE Conventions of a number of the States, having at the time of their adopting the Constitution, expressed a desire, in order to prevent misconstruction or abuse of its powers, that further declaratory and restrictive clauses should be added: And as extending the ground of public confidence in the Government, will best ensure the beneficent ends of its institution.

RESOLVED by the Senate and House of Representatives of the United States of America, in Congress assembled, two thirds of both Houses concurring, that the following Articles be proposed to the Legislatures of the several States, as amendments to the Constitution of the United States, all, or any of which Articles, when ratified by three fourths of the said Legislatures, to be valid to all intents and purposes, as part of the said Constitution; viz.

ARTICLES in addition to, and Amendment of the Constitution of the United States of American, proposed by Congress, and ratified by the

11 The first ten amendments (the Bill of Rights) were passed by Congress September 25, 1789, and ratified December 15, 1791.

Legislatures of the several States, pursuant to the fifth Article of the original Constitution.

I

Congress shall make no law respecting an establishment of religion, or prohibiting the free exercise thereof; or abridging the freedom of speech, or of the press; or the right of the people peaceably to assemble, and to petition the government for a redress of grievances.

II

A well-regulated militia, being necessary to the security of a free state, the right of the people to keep and bear arms, shall not be infringed.

III

No soldier shall, in time of peace be quartered in any house, without the consent of the owner, nor in time of war, but in a manner to be prescribed by law.

IV

The right of the people to be secure in their persons, houses, papers, and effects, against unreasonable searches and seizures, shall not be violated, and no warrants shall issue, but upon probable cause, supported by oath or affirmation, and particularly describing the place to be searched, and the persons or things to be seized.

V

No person shall be held to answer for a capital, or otherwise infamous crime, unless on a presentment or indictment of a grand jury, except in cases arising in the land or naval forces, or in the militia, when in actual service in time of war or public danger; nor shall any person be subject for the same offense to be twice put in jeopardy of life or limb; nor shall be compelled in any criminal case to be a witness against himself, nor be deprived of life, liberty, or property, without due process of law; nor shall private property be taken for public use, without just compensation.

VI

In all criminal prosecutions, the accused shall enjoy the right to a speedy and public trial, by an impartial jury of the state and district wherein the crime shall have been committed, which district shall have been previously ascertained by law, and to be informed of the nature and cause of the accusation; to be confronted with the witnesses against him; to have compulsory process for obtaining witnesses in his favor, and to have the assistance of counsel for his defense.

VII

In suits at common law, where the value in controversy shall exceed twenty dollars, the right of trial by jury shall be preserved, and no fact tried by a jury, shall be otherwise reexamined in any court of the United States, than according to the rules of the common law.

VIII

Excessive bail shall not be required, nor excessive fines imposed, nor cruel and unusual punishments inflicted.

IX

The enumeration in the Constitution, of certain rights, shall not be construed to deny or disparage others retained by the people.

X

The powers not delegated to the United States by the Constitution, nor prohibited by it to the states, are reserved to the states respectively, or to the people.

XI

The judicial power of the United States shall not be construed to extend to any suit in law or equity, commenced or prosecuted against one of the United States by citizens of another state, or by citizens or subjects of any foreign state.

Passed by Congress March 4, 1794. Ratified February 7, 1795

XII

The electors shall meet in their respective states and vote by ballot for President and Vice-President, one of whom, at least, shall not be an inhabitant of the same state with themselves; they shall name in their ballots the person voted for as President, and in distinct ballots the person voted for as Vice-President, and they shall make distinct lists of all persons voted for as President, and of all persons voted for as Vice-President, and of the number of votes for each, which lists they shall sign and certify, and transmit sealed to the seat of the government of the United States, directed to the President of the Senate;–The President of the Senate shall, in the presence of the Senate and House of Representatives, open all the certificates and the votes shall then be counted;–the person having the greatest number of votes for President, shall be the President, if such number be a majority of the whole number of electors appointed; and if no person have such majority, then from the persons having the highest numbers not exceeding three on the list of those voted for as President, the House of Representatives shall choose immediately, by ballot, the President. But in choosing the President, the votes shall be taken by states, the representation from each state having one vote; a quorum for this purpose shall consist of a member or members from two-thirds of the states, and a majority of all the states shall be necessary to a choice. [And if the House of Representatives shall not choose a President whenever the right of choice shall devolve upon them, before the fourth day of March next following, then the Vice-President shall act as President, as in the case of the death or other constitutional disability of the President.][12] The person having the greatest number of votes as Vice-President, shall be the Vice-President, if such number be a majority of the whole number of electors appointed, and if no person have a majority, then from the two highest numbers on the list, the Senate shall choose the Vice-President; a quorum for the purpose shall consist of two-thirds of the whole number of Senators, and a majority of the whole number shall be necessary to a choice. But no person constitutionally ineligible to the office of President shall be eligible to that of Vice-President of the United States.

Passed by Congress December 9, 1803. Ratified June 15, 1804.

XIII

Section 1. Neither slavery nor involuntary servitude, except as a punishment for crime whereof the party shall have been duly convicted, shall exist within the United States, or any place subject to their jurisdiction.

Section 2. Congress shall have power to enforce this article by appropriate legislation.

Passed by Congress January 31, 1865. Ratified December 6, 1865.

12 Superseded by section 3 of the Twentieth Amendment.

XIV

Section 1. All persons born or naturalized in the United States, and subject to the jurisdiction thereof, are citizens of the United States and of the state wherein they reside. No state shall make or enforce any law which shall abridge the privileges or immunities of citizens of the United States; nor shall any state deprive any person of life, liberty, or property, without due process of law; nor deny to any person within its jurisdiction the equal protection of the laws.

Section 2. Representatives shall be apportioned among the several states according to their respective numbers, counting the whole number of persons in each state, excluding Indians not taxed. But when the right to vote at any election for the choice of electors for President and Vice President of the United States, Representatives in Congress, the executive and judicial officers of a state, or the members of the legislature thereof, is denied to any of the male inhabitants of such state, being twenty-one years of age, and citizens of the United States, or in any way abridged, except for participation in rebellion, or other crime, the basis of representation therein shall be reduced in the proportion which the number of such male citizens shall bear to the whole number of male citizens twenty-one years of age in such state.

Section 3. No person shall be a Senator or Representative in Congress, or elector of President and Vice President, or hold any office, civil or military, under the United States, or under any state, who, having previously taken an oath, as a member of Congress, or as an officer of the United States, or as a member of any state legislature, or as an executive or judicial officer of any state, to support the Constitution of the United States, shall have engaged in insurrection or rebellion against the same, or given aid or comfort to the enemies thereof. But Congress may by a vote of two-thirds of each House, remove such disability.

Section 4. The validity of the public debt of the United States, authorized by law, including debts incurred for payment of pensions and bounties for services in suppressing insurrection or rebellion, shall not be questioned. But neither the United States nor any state shall assume or pay any debt or obligation incurred in aid of insurrection or rebellion against the United States, or any claim for the loss or emancipation of any slave; but all such debts, obligations and claims shall be held illegal and void.

Section 5. The Congress shall have power to enforce, by appropriate legislation, the provisions of this article.

Passed by Congress June 13, 1866. Ratified July 9, 1868

XV

Section 1. The right of citizens of the United States to vote shall not be denied or abridged by the United States or by any state on account of race, color, or previous condition of servitude.

Section 2. The Congress shall have power to enforce this article by appropriate legislation.

Passed by Congress February 26, 1869. Ratified February 3, 1870.

XVI

The Congress shall have power to lay and collect taxes on incomes, from whatever source derived, without apportionment among the several states, and without regard to any census of enumeration.

Passed by Congress July 2, 1909. Ratified February 3, 1913.

XVII

The Senate of the United States shall be composed of two Senators from each state, elected by the people thereof, for six years; and each Senator shall have one vote. The electors in each state shall have the qualifications requisite for electors of the most numerous branch of the state legislatures.

When vacancies happen in the representation of any state in the Senate, the executive authority of such state shall issue writs of election to fill such vacancies: Provided, that the legislature of any state may empower the executive thereof to make temporary appointments until the people fill the vacancies by election as the legislature may direct.

This amendment shall not be so construed as to affect the election or term of any Senator chosen before it becomes valid as part of the Constitution.

Passed by Congress May 13, 1912. Ratified April 8, 1913.

XVIII

Section 1. After one year from the ratification of this article the manufacture, sale, or transportation of intoxicating liquors within, the importation thereof into, or the exportation thereof from the United States and all territory subject to the jurisdiction thereof for beverage purposes is hereby prohibited.

Section 2. The Congress and the several states shall have concurrent power to enforce this article by appropriate legislation.

Section 3. This article shall be inoperative unless it shall have been ratified as an amendment to the Constitution by the legislatures of the several states, as provided in the Constitution, within seven years from the date of the submission hereof to the states by the Congress.

Passed by Congress December 18, 1917. Ratified January 16, 1919.

Repealed by Amendment 21.

XIX

The right of citizens of the United States to vote shall not be denied or abridged by the United States or by any state on account of sex.

Congress shall have power to enforce this article by appropriate legislation.

Passed by Congress June 4, 1919. Ratified August 18, 1920.

XX

Section 1. The terms of the President and Vice President shall end at noon on the 20th day of January, and the terms of Senators and Representatives at noon on the 3rd day of January, of the years in which such terms would have ended if this article had not been ratified; and the terms of their successors shall then begin.

Section 2. The Congress shall assemble at least once in every year, and such meeting shall begin at noon on the 3d day of January, unless they shall by law appoint a different day.

Section 3. If, at the time fixed for the beginning of the term of the President, the President elect shall have died, the Vice President elect shall become President. If a President shall not have been chosen before the time fixed for the beginning of his term, or if the President elect shall have failed to qualify, then the Vice President elect shall act as President until a President shall have qualified; and the Congress may by law provide for the case wherein neither a President elect nor a Vice President elect shall have qualified, declaring who shall then act as President, or the manner in which one who is to act shall be selected, and such person shall act accordingly until a President or Vice President shall have qualified.

Section 4. The Congress may by law provide for the case of the death of any of the persons from whom the House of Representatives may choose a President whenever the right of choice shall have devolved upon them, and for the case of the death of any of the persons from whom the Senate may choose a Vice President whenever the right of choice shall have devolved upon them.

Section 5. Sections 1 and 2 shall take effect on the 15th day of October following the ratification of this article.

Section 6. This article shall be inoperative unless it shall have been ratified as an amendment to the Constitution by the legislatures of three-fourths of the several states within seven years from the date of its submission.

Passed by Congress March 2, 1932. Ratified January 23, 1933.

XXI

Section 1. The eighteenth article of amendment to the Constitution of the United States is hereby repealed.

Section 2. The transportation or importation into any state, territory, or possession of the United States for delivery or use therein of intoxicating liquors, in violation of the laws thereof, is hereby prohibited.

Section 3. This article shall be inoperative unless it shall have been ratified as an amendment to the Constitution by conventions in the several states, as provided in the Constitution, within seven years from the date of the submission hereof to the states by the Congress.

Passed by Congress February 20, 1933. Ratified December 5, 1933.

XXII

Section 1. No person shall be elected to the office of the President more than twice, and no person who has held the office of President, or acted as President, for more than two years of a term to which some other person was elected President shall be elected to the office of the President more than once. But this article shall not apply to any person holding the office of President when this article was proposed by the Congress, and shall not prevent any person who may be holding the office of President, or acting as President, during the term within which this article becomes operative from holding the office of President or acting as President during the remainder of such term.

Section 2. This article shall be inoperative unless it shall have been ratified as an amendment to the Constitution by the legislatures of three-fourths of the several states within seven years from the date of its submission to the states by the Congress.

Passed by Congress March 21, 1947. Ratified February 27, 1951.

XXIII

Section 1. The District constituting the seat of government of the United States shall appoint in such manner as the Congress may direct:

A number of electors of President and Vice President equal to the whole number of Senators and Representatives in Congress to which the District would be entitled if it were a state, but in no event more than the least populous state; they shall be in addition to those appointed by the states, but they shall be considered, for the purposes of the election of President and Vice President, to be electors appointed by a state; and they shall meet in the District and perform such duties as provided by the twelfth article of amendment.

Section 2. The Congress shall have power to enforce this article by appropriate legislation.

Passed by Congress June 16, 1960. Ratified March 29, 1961.

XXIV

Section 1. The right of citizens of the United States to vote in any primary or other election for President or Vice President, for electors for President or Vice President, or for Senator or Representative in Congress, shall not be denied or abridged by the United States or any state by reason of failure to pay any poll tax or other tax.

Section 2. The Congress shall have power to enforce this article by appropriate legislation.

Passed by Congress August 27, 1962. Ratified January 23, 1964.

XXV

Section 1. In case of the removal of the President from office or of his death or resignation, the Vice President shall become President.

Section 2. Whenever there is a vacancy in the office of the Vice President, the President shall nominate a Vice President who shall take office upon confirmation by a majority vote of both Houses of Congress.

Section 3. Whenever the President transmits to the President pro tempore of the Senate and the Speaker of the House of Representatives his written declaration that he is unable to discharge the powers and duties of his office, and until he transmits to them a written declaration to the contrary, such powers and duties shall be discharged by the Vice President as Acting President.

Section 4. Whenever the Vice President and a majority of either the principal officers of the executive departments or of such other body as Congress may by law provide, transmit to the President pro tempore of the Senate and the Speaker of the House of Representatives their written declaration that the President is unable to discharge the powers and duties of his office, the Vice President shall immediately assume the powers and duties of the office as Acting President.

Thereafter, when the President transmits to the President pro tempore of the Senate and the Speaker of the House of Representatives his written declaration that no inability exists, he shall resume the powers and duties of his office unless the Vice President and a majority of either the principal officers of the executive department or of such other body as Congress may by law provide, transmit within four days to the President pro tempore of the Senate and the Speaker of the House of Representatives their written declaration that the President is unable to discharge the powers and duties of his office. Thereupon Congress shall decide the issue, assembling within forty-eight hours for that purpose if not in session. If the Congress, within twenty-one days after receipt of the latter written declaration, or, if Congress is not in session, within twenty-one days after Congress is required to assemble, determines by two-thirds vote of both Houses that the President is unable to discharge the powers and duties of his office, the Vice President shall continue to discharge the same as Acting President; otherwise, the President shall resume the powers and duties of his office.

Passed by Congress July 6, 1965. Ratified February 10, 1967.

XXVI

Section 1. The right of citizens of the United States, who are 18 years of age or older, to vote, shall not be denied or abridged by the United States or any state on account of age.

Section 2. The Congress shall have the power to enforce this article by appropriate legislation.

Passed by Congress March 23, 1971. Ratified July 1, 1971.

XXVII

No law varying the compensation for the services of the Senators and Representatives shall take effect until an election of Representatives shall have intervened.

Congress submitted the text of the Twenty-Seventh Amendment to the States as part of the proposed Bill of Rights on September 25, 1789. The Amendment was not ratified together with the first ten Amendments, which became effective on December 15, 1791. The Twenty-Seventh Amendment was ratified on May 7, 1992, by the vote of Michigan.

ABOUT THE AUTHOR

MILTON J. NIEUWSMA is a two-time Emmy Award-winning writer and creator of the PBS series *Inventing America: Conversations with the Founders.* He and his wife, Marilee, have three children and seven grandchilden and live in Holland, Michigan.

For sales, editorial information, subsidiary rights information or a catalog, please write or phone or e-mail

IBOOKS
Manhanset House
Shelter Island Hts., New York 11965, US
Tel: 212-427-7139
www.BrickTowerPress.com
bricktower@aol.com
www.IngramContent.com

For sales in the UK and Europe please contact our distributor

Gazelle Book Services
White Cross Mills
Lancaster, LA1 4XS, UK
Tel: (01524) 68765 Fax: (01524) 63232
email: jacky@gazellebooks.co.uk

For a DVDs of "Inventing America" please contact

WGVU/PBS
301 Fulton St. W
Grand Rapids, MI 49504, U.S.
Tel: 800-442-2771 Fax 616-331-6625
www.wgvu.org

To access "Inventing America" on the web go to www.inventing-america.org